WRITING SKILLS FOR TECHNICAL PURPOSES

WRITING SKILLS FOR TECHNICAL PURPOSES

Editor
Rajmohan Joshi

ISHA

ISHA BOOKS
DELHI-110033

Writing Skills for Technical Purposes

ISBN: 81-8205-378-1

Rs. 690

Published in 2006 in India by
Isha Books
D-43, Prithviraj Road, Adarsh Nagar, Delhi-110033
E-mail : ishabooks@hotmail.com

Laser Typesetting at: Master Computers, Delhi
Printed at: Salasar Imaging System, Delhi

Preface

In a world of rapid technological development, people are constantly falling behind and becoming technological illiterates. Technology companies are constantly struggling to find effective ways to help customers or potential customers understand the advantages or the operation of their new products. Technical writing is a specialised, structured way of writing, where information is presented in a format and manner that best suits the cognitive and psychological needs of the readers, so they can respond to a document as its author intended and achieve the purpose related to that document. Thus, it is writing formatted and shaped to make reading as simple, poignant, unequivocal, and enjoyable as possible. It so happens that most technical writing positions are still primarily offered to those who can write effective end-user manuals, system design documents, Web sites, and the like for engineering and IT firms.

Technical writing, a subset of technical communication, is used in fields as diverse as computer hardware and software, chemistry, the aerospace industry, robotics, consumer electronics, and biotechnology. At the beginning of a project, the technical writer identifies the audience for the documentation. For example, a writer might be documenting a VCR for a nontechnical man of average literacy who needs to know how to set the time and tape television shows, or for a technician who must diagnose, repair, or replace internal components. Technical writing is most often associated with online Help and user manuals;

however, there are other forms of technical content created by technical writers.

A good technical writer can write about a complicated technical subject or task in ways that almost anyone can understand. Precision in technical writing tends to be critical because if anything is described incorrectly, readers may act improperly on what is said, causing mistakes and problems at work. Technical writers often have a certified degree in English, technical writing, the technical field for which they are writing, or a combination of these. It is most important that they have enough expertise to understand their audience's background and needs.

This book aims to teach students the skill of technical writing. It is unique in that it gets to the point, uses practical outlines throughout, and actually shows students how to produce the most common technical documents step-by-step. It employs a laid-back approach that is focused on providing real-world information in a straightforward and easy-to-understand manner.

Editor

Contents

1

Technical Writing

The term "technical" refers to knowledge that is not widespread, that is more the territory of experts and specialists. In a world of rapid technological development, people are constantly falling behind and becoming technological illiterates. Technology companies are constantly struggling to find effective ways to help customers or potential customers understand the advantages or the operation of their new products.

Technical writing is a specialized, structured Way of writing, where information is Presented in a format and manner that best suits the cognitive and psychological needs of the readers, so they can respond to a document as its author intended and achieve the purpose related to that document. Thus, it is writing formatted and shaped to make reading as simple, poignant, unequivocal, and enjoyable as possible (i.e., "user friendly"). It so happens that most technical writing positions are still primarily offered to those who can write effective end-user manuals, system design documents, Web sites, and the like for engineering and IT firms.

Technical writing, a subset of technical communication, is used in fields as diverse as computer hardware and software, chemistry, the aerospace industry, robotics, consumer electronics, and biotechnology. At the beginning of a project, the technical writer identifies the audience for the documentation. For example, a writer might be documenting a VCR for a nontechnical American of average literacy who needs to know how to set the time and tape television shows, or for a technician who must diagnose, repair, or replace internal components.

Technical writing is most often associated with online Help and user manuals; however, there are other forms of technical content created by technical writers, including:

— White papers

— User guides

— Reference documents

— Training materials

— Installation guides

— Troubleshooting guides

— Specifications

— Proposals

— Magazine articles

— Policies and Procedures

— Requirements documentation

— Certification and Accreditation activities

— Procedures

How one writes is as important as What one writes. So, language itself is important to enable readers to understand and believe the written text. Language impacts a reader's ability to comprehend and assimilate what a writer is presenting. Furthermore, people can, and do, judge things by outward appearances all the time, it is essential to make good impressions when communicating in a business setting. When one communicates (whether writing, giving a speech, or talking on the phone) information must be presented effectively and to a large degree, attractively.

These elements strongly affect perceived writer and organizational credibility and professionalism -- highly sought after commodities for individual and organizational success. Format, organization, and style are important in that they make information available, accessible, and readable. Format and the like are the "how" of a written presentation. Format choices can give a document the highly sought after technical or business "look" organizations hope for. In essence, this is part of "corporate identity" promotion.

Technical Communication

Technical communications is the delivery of technical information to readers (or listeners or viewers) in a manner that is adapted to their needs, level of understanding, and background. In fact, this audience element is so important that it is one of the cornerstones of this course: you are challenged to write about highly technical subjects but in a way that a beginner-a nonspecialist-could understand. This ability to "translate" technical information to nonspecialists is a key skill to any technical communicator.

Technical communication is the process of conveying information about technology to an intended audience. A technical communicator is a person whose job involves technical communication. Technical communication jobs include the following:

— Technical writer

— Technical editor

— Information architect

— Usability expert

— User interface designer

— Technical artist

— Technical trainer

The technology can be of any kind, including the sciences, high technology including computers and software, consumer electronics, and so on.

Technical Writer

A good technical writer can write about a complicated technical subject or task in ways that almost anyone can understand. Precision in technical writing tends to be critical because if anything is described incorrectly, readers may act improperly on what is said, causing mistakes and problems at work. Technical writers often have a certified degree in English, technical writing, the technical field for which they are writing, or a combination of these.

It is most important that they have enough expertise to understand their audience's background and needs. For example, writers who develop documentation for software APIs, microcontroller operation, and other technical subjects are often paid more than those who write guides for a nontechnical audience (for example, how to use email), because it is difficult to find good writers with advanced technical knowledge.

After the documentation is written, using a desktop publishing tool or a help authoring tool, it is normally reviewed for accuracy by one or more "Subject Matter Experts" (SMEs). Technical Writers are known in United Kingdom and some other countries as Technical Authors. A technical writer is a person who creates documentation for a technology. They are responsible for writing text that is accurate, readable, accessible, and helpful to its intended audience. Technical writing, a subset of technical communication, is used in fields as diverse as chemistry, the aerospace industry, robotics, consumer electronic products such as VCRs or digital cameras, biotechnology, software, computer hardware, and many others.

At the beginning of a project, the technical writer identifies the audience for the documentation. For example, if documenting a VCR, the writer must determine whether the audience is a nontechnical American of average literacy who needs to know how to set the time and tape television shows, or a technician who must diagnose, repair, or replace internal components. Technical writers often have a degree in English, technical writing, the technical field for which they are writing, or a combination of these.

It is most important that they have enough expertise to understand their audience's background and needs. For example, writers who develop documentation for software APIs, microcontroller operation, and other technical subjects are often paid more than those who write guides for a nontechnical audience (for example, how to use email), because it is difficult to find good writers with advanced technical knowledge. After the documentation is written, using a desktop publishing tool or a help authoring tool, it is normally reviewed for accuracy by one or more "subject matter experts" (SMEs).

Technical Writing

Writing well is difficult and time-consuming, and writing in a technical way and about technical subjects compounds the difficulties. The entire point of communications is to disseminate useful information. To be useful, information must be understood and acted upon. Fortunately, tools and techniques are available to make writing more accessible and easy to understand.]Effective communications require quality content, language, format, and more. The entire point of communications is to disseminate information; this is where written content comes in. To present the appropriate content, it is imperative to understand one's audience and writing purpose.

If a document does not communicate the information that the writer intends and what he or she wants the reader to understand, then the communication is meaningless. The writer has a self-interest in making the extra effort: Looking credible is as important as being credible and getting results in business. Respect and credibility of the writer/speaker are integral to effective communications. Readers will not trust the information from an author if they do not believe that author is a valuable source of information or the purveyor of worthwhile ideas. Furthermore, being respected is essential to being persuasive, a key ingredient in business.

Technical Document

A document is a writing that contains information. Traditionally, the medium of a document was paper and the information was applied to it as ink either by hand (to make a hand-written document) or by a mechanical process (such as a printing press or a laser printer). Through time, documents have also been written with ink on papyrus (starting in ancient Egypt) or parchment, scratched as runes on stone using a sharp apparatus, stamped or cut into clay and baked to make clay tablets (i.e. in Sumerian and Mesopotamic civilisations). Paper, papyrus or parchment might be rolled up as scrolls or cut into sheets and bound into books.

Stacks of clay tablets might also be thought of as books. Small documents might also be stapled. Today, electronic means for storing and displaying documents are also popular; a variety of computers and displays can be used, for example:

— a desktop computer with a monitor

— a laptop

— a Personal Digital Assistant

— refreshable electronic paper

Most technical writing in day-to-day business involves the preparation of various "reports" (Fig. 1). Writing reports is common for many technical people because reports are a major part of the development and application of technology. Very few companies pay technical professionals a salary without written words to implement and evaluate what has been worked on or developed. For example, if an engineer spends a year developing a new transmission for a car, several types of reports are needed for the design, evaluation, and implementation of the new component.

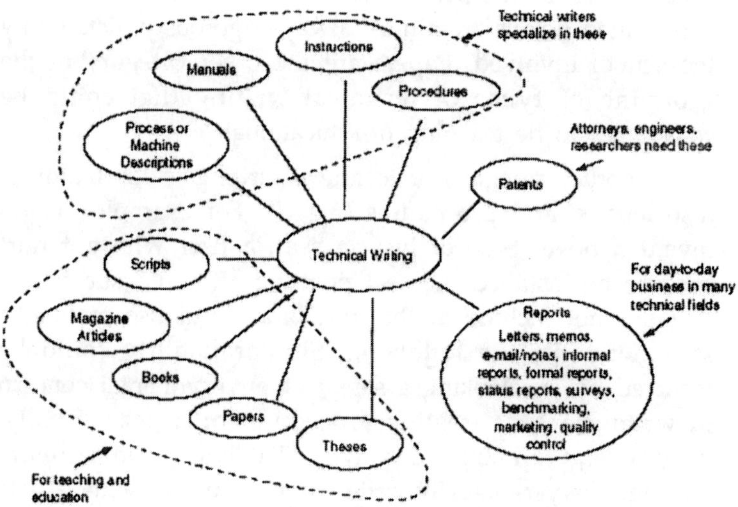

Figure 1. Spectrum of technical writing

Engineering must also report to management on the viability of design, costs, and work objectives. This usually requires a written document and related engineering drawings-a report. A second category of technical writing includes documents for teaching and education (Fig. 1) in the form of scripts, magazine articles, books, papers, and degree theses. Scripts for videos, movies, magazine articles, or multimedia presentations are most often written and edited by professionals in these fields. Books on technical topics are most often written by academicians, although technical professionals occasionally may write an entire book in their area of experience and knowledge.

Writing a book obviously requires much more discipline than the writing of reports, but it still requires the clarity of presentation and purpose as in the reports and papers of day-today business. Papers and theses are more common forms of educational or informational documents written by technical professionals. Of course, many people in science and engineering write theses. However, they usually only do one per degree, and the formal writing style and related details are almost always rigorously dictated by the school involved. Papers are the other category in the grouping of types of technical writing that could be considered to be teaching or educational.

Another category of technical writing is for manuals, instructions, and procedures (Fig. 1). For example, if you invent a novel type of bicycle seat, a user who got hurt because he installed the seat pointing aft could sue you if you did not include in the installation and use manual a statement like the following: Similar liability could be incurred by overlooking a safety or environmental concern in writing a heat treating procedure for a gear. Finally, patents require another key type of document in technical writing. Lawyers usually write patents, but not without lots of writing and searching on the part of the applicant. Thus, this book addresses the inventor's part of a patent application and the general criteria for patentability.

Attributes of Technical Writing

In general, technical writing has a degree of formality, and it generally focuses on a specific subject with the purpose of making something happen or sharing useful information or knowledge. Ten general attributes of technical writing are listed and described in the following sections:

- — It pertains to a technical subject.
- — It has a purpose.
- — It has an objective.
- — It conveys information/facts/data.
- — It is impersonal.
- — It is concise.
- — It is directed.
- — It is performed with a particular style and in a particular format.
- — It is archival.
- — It cites contributions of others.

There are probably more attributes, but the attributes in the above list define some key characteristics that distinguish technical writing from other types of writing. Technical writing must pertain to some aspect of engineering or the sciences in a given subject area such as the following:

- — Philosophy, psychology, and religion
- — History
- — Geography and anthropology
- — Social sciences
- — Political science
- — Law
- — Education
- — Fine arts
- — Language and literature
- — Science
- — Agriculture

— Technology

— Health/medicine

Libraries usually categorize books into these subject categories, and technical writing may apply to any of these categories if the work contains engineering or science as the focus. For example, a paper on the acoustic/sound aspects of a piano could be very technical and end up in the music category. Similarly, a book on restoration techniques for antiques could be rife with chemistry and metallurgy, but it may end up in the fine arts category. The point is that technical writing can be on one of many different subjects if the subject is being described or evaluated in an objective fashion.

A technical document always is written for a reason, and the purpose of reports may be to explain what was done, why it was done, and/or the results of a study. The purpose of reports on investigations is usually to present the results of the study. The purpose of reports and papers should also be clearly stated, as in the following example: This excerpt identifies the purpose of the report as the presentation of results from a statistical study. Readers are also informed why the author(s) did the work. If the report is done correctly, it will also close with recommendations on what should happen next.

The objective of a technical report is the overall reason for doing the work. In an industrial situation, the objective of any work is usually to make or increase profits. In the preceding example, the objective was to reduce failure rates to a level of less than three ppm. Technical writing should have substance in every statement. If a sentence does not convey information pertinent to a study, leave it out. Technical writing is focused on the technology under discussion. A report without facts or scientific evidence to support an opinion also usually lacks credibility, and it is likely to be unsuccessful in achieving its purpose and objective. The following report excerpt illustrates reports with and without data. The use of data and factual information makes the work a technical report.

The communication without the data is not much different than a water cooler discussion between coworkers. If the author is the leading expert of the world on grinding, his or her opinions may make the report persuasive, but most people are not infallible authorities on subjects. Most reports need facts or data to support conclusions and recommendations, and the verbs listed here are probably associated with factual statements:

— Determined

— Solved

— Built

— Accepted

— Rejected

— Completed

— Passed

— Failed

— Broke

— Approved

— Cancelled

— Invented

— Designed

— Developed

— Discovered

— Uncovered

— Deduced

— Studied

Verbs that are often not associated with factual statements include words like the following:

— Think

— May be

— Suggest

— Appear

— Suppose

Impersonal Voice

The use of first person pronouns is usually discouraged in technical writing. The intrusion of "I" makes the work less authoritative. Similarly, it is inappropriate to use names of people and/or trade names unless there is no other way to describe the item. The preceding excerpt from a report on metal hardness problems illustrates how not to write a technical report. Judicious use of personal pronouns is acceptable, but because a novice in technical writing may not know when it is acceptable, it is probably advisable to avoid the use of personal pronouns (I, you, me, we, mine) in formal reports and published papers.

Writing in the third person is the style adopted in many journals and organizations. With regard to using people's names in reports, it is not necessary and it reads "unprofessional." In addition, it adds length, and anything that adds unnecessary length to a document should not be done. If the intent of including names is to give credit, the correct placement of credits is not in the body of a report. Personal pronouns and names should be omitted because they are unnecessary. Trade names should be avoided because of liability considerations. The message can usually be conveyed fully without their use:

Be Concise: Technical reports are usually written for business reasons. They are not intended to entertain; they communicate information to an identified person or group.

Say what you want to say and get out! Wandering sentences and extra words reflect badly on the author and often have a negative effect on the readership that you are trying to reach.

Concision can become an acquired writing trait. There are text books on the subject, but a major source of extra words are phrases such as "it follows that," "in any case," and "nonetheless." It is often possible to replace these phrases with a punctuation mark.

Style and Format

The attributes of technical writing also include style and format. Style is the way that you write; format is the ordering and physical layout of a document. The appropriate style for technical writing is objective. Technical documents present data, facts, calculations, test results, and theories, and these must be presented in an accurate manner that is not opinionated. Conclusions are inferred from test results; recommendations are the logical outcome of the conclusions. The format (the basic elements and their placement) of technical papers and reports is a more structured one than that used for other forms of writing. Formal technical reports have basic elements and a structure as follows:

- Introduction (why you are doing the work)
- Procedure (what you did)
- Results (what happened)
- Discussion (what it means)
- Conclusions (what was learned)
- Recommendations (what is to be done with the new information or knowledge)

This style and format have been agreed to by international technical journals, most educational institutions that teach in English, and most industries or organizations that employ engineers and scientists.

Archival

An intrinsic part of the value of technical writing is that it is written in such a manner that it can be archived and produce valuable and usable information in the future. Conversely, technical documents should not be generated on transient issues or subjects that will not be pertinent in the future. In the first example, the problem machines were slated to be scrapped, so there may not be a need to archive the report on the details of the shutdown.

In the latter case, the problem was due to a fixture error. This kind of problem could reoccur. There is probably value in archiving this document. Most businesses and industries have guidelines on how long various documents need to be saved, and, if a technical paper is published in an archived journal, the document will be available for as long as the journal is kept in libraries. Thus, technical writing often results in documents that have value in the future and should be archived.

Attributions

Formal technical reports and papers must show sources of information and recognize contributions of others. Formal reports also provide the opportunity to cite contributions or funding in an acknowledgment section at the end of a report. In summary, the proper use and citation of the work of others is another attribute that sets technical writing apart from other types of writing.

Other Types of Writing

In general, technical writing has a degree of formality, and it generally focuses on a specific subject. Reports and other technical documents are written to share useful information and knowledge or to make something happen. Technical writing should have substance in every statement. Technical writing also has a style and structure that sets it apart from other types of writing. Most important of these characteristics is that it be objective and supported by facts and data and that every attempt is made to ensure that the information is correct.

The most writing that some people will do in their lives is during their formal education. We learn the basics in grade school and practice this skill in the remainder of our schooling in countless themes, essays, term papers and [shudder] exams with essay questions. This type of writing may be termed "school writing." The teacher dictates the format. Each teacher wants certain elements, and, as we all have learned the hard way, your writing had better conform. In the working world, industry, business, and health, there are no Notre Dame nuns to tell you how to write. If your company does not mandate a format and style, you must make the decisions.

Each writer does something different as does each magazine, each newspaper, and each essayist. Technical writing, on the other hand, is done with a singular style and format that describes:

— Why you are doing the work (introduction)

— What you did (procedure)

— What happened (results)

— What it means (discussion)

— What was learned (conclusions)

— What is to be done with the results (recommendations)

Instructions

Instructions for use of a product or a process are often considered technical writing. They are often pertaining to a technology, and they are written in a style that has many of the attributes of technical writing.

Advertising

This writing is not considered technical writing because it is not factual. The claim of "best" could only be substantiated by testing every tool in the world using every possible test criterion. "Superior" statements pervade advertising on all types of products and services. Superlatives almost never can be substantiated, and thus they are not factual and should not be a part of technical writing.

Creative Writing

Creative writing requires saying things in words that create illusions or that establish a mood or other desired affect. It can be just humorous or entertaining like a murder mystery. A characteristic of this type of writing is the use of expressive and descriptive language. Poetry (an acquired taste) also fits within this category of writing.

Personal opinions are not part of technical writing. They belong on the editorial pages of newspapers. Opinions and fads may also cross into technical subjects. For example, business and finance publications can be based on economic theories and mathematics, and thus they could be considered technical writing. However, many business books on management are mostly opinions rather than fact. Even many books in the hard sciences, like physics and biology, are based more on subjective interpretations. These forms of writing are not classified as technical writing.

Documents that convey information can be technical writing if the information has the technical writing attributes. The following example of a meeting notification is certainly not part of technical writing. The program chairperson would probably archive the note for his or her annual report, but otherwise this meeting announcement would have no value as a technical document to others. Newspapers and news magazines also convey information. Most are not technical writing because they usually do not address issues in engineering or science. Newsletters, similarly, often do not match the attributes of technical writing.

Most employees in large firms receive several memos or e-mails like the following each day. They are from bosses, secretaries, teammates, and colleagues; they deal with administrative matters such as meetings, deadlines, safety issues, and so forth. They seldom match the attributes of technical writing.

Much writing is intended simply for the entertainment of the reader. Countless books and magazines have reader entertainment as their primary objective. This is not technical writing. Stories and novels may not be factual. The information is often made up. Even books on real events may not pertain to technical writing when the purpose is to entertain rather than to serve a scientific purpose. For example, biographies and novels on real incidents usually do not pertain to engineering and science. Even those that do are often not technical writing, because their objective is to entertain, amuse, or engage readers. The same applies to business and finance publications. Some books on technical topics are written in a way to entertain or capture the imagination of readers. This form of writing is not technical writing.

2

Writing Process

Peer-reviewing

Peer-reviewing is a good way to become a better writer because it provides experience in looking critically at writing. It means People getting together to read, comment on, and recommend improvements on each other's work. It also known as peer-editing.

At the beginning of a peer review, provide your peer-reviewers with notes on the writing assignment and on your goals and concerns about your writing project. Alert reviewers to these problems; make it clear what kinds of things you were trying to do. Similarly, ask writers whose work you are peer-reviewing to supply you with information on their objectives and concerns.

When you peer-review other people's writing, remember above all that you should consider all aspects of that writing, not just—in fact, least of all—the grammar, spelling, and punctuation. If you are new to peer-reviewing, you may forget to review the draft for certain aspects:

— Make sure that your review is comprehensive. Consider all aspects of the draft you're reviewing, not just the grammar, punctuation, and spelling.

— Read the draft several times, looking for high-level matters such as interest level, persuasiveness, general organization, and clarity of discussion in your first reading.

— Be careful about making comments or criticisms that are based on your own personal style. Base your criticisms and suggestions for improvements on generally accepted guidelines, concepts, and rules. If you do make a comment that is really your own preference, explain it.

— Explain the problems you find fully. Don't just say a paper "seems disorganized." Explain what is disorganized about it. Use specific details from the draft to demonstrate your case.

— Whenever you criticize something in the writer's draft, try to suggest some way to correct the problem. It's not enough to tell the writer that her paper seems disorganized, for example. Explain how that problem could be solved.

— Base your comments and criticisms on accepted guidelines, concepts, principles, and rules. It's not enough to tell a writer that two paragraphs ought to be switched, for example. State the reason why: more general, introductory information should come first, for example.

— Avoid rewriting the draft that you are reviewing. In your efforts to suggest improvements and corrections, don't go overboard and rewrite the draft yourself. Doing so steals from the original writer the opportunity to learn and improve as a writer.

— Find positive, encouraging things to say about the draft you're reviewing. Compliments, even small ones, are usually wildly appreciated. Read through the draft at least once looking for things that were done well, and then let the writer know about them.

Phases of Reviewing

— Organize a writing team, if necessary or possible

— Review how well the draft is adapted to its audience

— Assess how well the draft achieves its purpose

— Analyze whether the writing topic has been narrowed sufficiently

— Review the organization of the draft

— Check the content of the draft

— Review the coherence of the draft, that is, its use of transition techniques

— Analyze the title, introduction, and conclusion

— Review the use of topic sentences in the draft

— Analyze the draft for sentence style and clarity

— Check whether quotations, paraphrases, and summaries are handled correctly

— Review the handling of graphics, if they are used in the draft

— Review the documentation of the draft, that is, its method of handling source references and the works-cited list

— Check format details

— Check for grammar, punctuation, usage, and spelling problems

Once you've finished a peer review, it's a good idea to write a summary of your thoughts, observations, impressions, criticisms, or feelings about the rough draft. Notice in the note some of the following details:

— The comments are categorized according to type of problem or error--grammar and usage comments in one group; higher level comments on such as things content, organization, and interest-level in another group.

— Relative importance of the groups of comments is indicated. The peer-reviewer indicates which suggestions would be "nice" to incorporate, and which ones are critical to the success of the writing project.

— Most of the comments include some brief statement of guidelines, rules, examples, or common sense. The reviewer doesn't simply say "This is wrong; fix it." She also explains the basis for the comment.

— Questions are addressed to the writer. The reviewer is doublechecking to see if the writer really meant to state or imply certain things.

— The reviewer includes positive comments to make about the rough draft, and finds nonantagonistic, sympathetic ways to state criticisms.

Team-writing

Team-writing means people getting together to plan, write, and revise writing projects as a group, or team. Another name for this practice is collaborative writing-collaborative writing that is out in the open rather than under cover. It is known as plagiarism.

Team-writing is one of the common ways people in the worlds of business, government, science, and technology handle large writing projects. When you begin picking team members for a writing project, choose people with different backgrounds and interests. Just as a diverse, well-rounded background for an individual writer is an advantage, a group of diverse individuals makes for a well-rounded writing team. Once you've assembled your writing team, most of the work is the same as it would be if you were writing by yourself, except that each phases is a team effort. Specifically, meet with your team to decide or plan the following:

Much of the work in a team-writing project must be done by individual team members on their own.

— Have each team member responsible for the writing of one major section of the paper.

— Have each team member responsible for locating, reading, and taking notes on an equal part of the information sources.

Some of the work for the project that could be done as a team you may want to do first independently. For example, brainstorming, narrowing, and especially outlining should be done first be each team member on his own; then get together and compare notes. Keep in mind how group dynamics can unknowingly suppress certain ideas and how less assertive team members might be reluctant to contribute their valuable ideas in the group context. After you've divided up the work for the project, write a formal chart and distribute it to all the members.

Early in your team writing project, set up a schedule of key dates. This schedule will enable you and your team members to make steady, organized progress and complete the project on time. Include not only completion dates for key phases of the project but also meeting dates and the subject and purpose of those meetings. Notice these details about that schedule:

— Several meetings are scheduled in which members discuss the information they are finding or are not finding.

— Several meetings are scheduled to review the project details, specifically, the topic, audience, purpose, situation, and outline. As you learn more about the topic and become more settled in the project, your team may want to change some of these details or make them more specific.

— Several rough drafts are scheduled. Team members peer-review each other's drafts of individual sections twice, the second time to see if the recommended changes have worked. Once the complete draft is put together, it too is reviewed twice.

When you work as a team, there is always the chance that one of the team members, for whatever reason, may have more or less than a fair share of the workload. Therefore, it's important to find a way to keep track of what each team member is doing. A good way to do that is to have each team member keep a journal or log of what kind of work he does and how much time he spends doing it.

At the end of the project, if there are any problems in the balance of the work, the journal should make that fact very clear. At the end of the project, team members can add up their hours spent on the project; if anyone has spent a little more than her share of time working, the other members can make up for it by buying her dinner or some reward like that. Similarly, as you get down toward the end of the project, if it's clear from the journals that one team member's work responsibilities turned out, through no fault of his own, to be smaller than those of the others, he can make up for it by doing more of the finish-up work such as typing, proofing, or copying.

Because the individual sections will be written by different writers who are apt to have different writing styles, set up a style guide in which your team members list their agreements on how things are to be handled in the paper as a whole. Before you and your team members write the first rough drafts, you can't expect to cover every possible difference in style and format. Therefore, plan to update this style sheet when you review the rough drafts of the individual sections and, especially, when review the complete draft. Try to schedule as many reviews of your team's written work as possible.

A critical stage in team-writing a paper comes when you put together into one complete draft those individual sections written by different team members. It's then that you'll probably see how different in tone, treatment, and style each section is. You must as a group find a way to revise and edit the complete rough draft that will make it read consistently so that it won't be so obviously written by three or four different people. When you've finished with reviewing and revising, it's time for the finish-up work to get the draft ready to hand in. That work is the same as it would be if you were writing the paper on your own, only in this case the workloads can be divided up.

Analysis of Audience

The audience of a technical report – or any piece of writing for that matter – is the intended or potential reader or readers. For most technical writers, this is the most important consideration in planning, writing, and reviewing a document. You "adapt" your writing to meet the needs, interests, and background of the readers who will be reading your writing.

The principle seems absurdly simple and obvious. It's much the same as telling someone, "Talk so the person in front of you can understand what you're saying." It's like saying, "Don't talk rocket science to your six-year-old." But, in fact, lack of audience analysis and adaptation is one of the root causes of most of the problems you find in professional, technical documents – particularly instructions where it surfaces most glaringly.

Types of Audiences

One of the first things to do when you analyze and audience is to identify its type (or types--it's rarely just one type). The common division of audiences into categories is as follows:

— *Experts*: These are the people who know the theory and the product inside and out. They designed it, they tested it, they know everything about it. Often, they have advanced degrees and operate in academic settings or in research and development areas of the government and business worlds. The nonspecialist reader is least likely to understand what these people are saying-but also has the least reason to try. More often, the communication challenge faced by the expert is communicating to the technician and the executive.

— *Technicians*: These are the people who build, operate, maintain, and repair the stuff that the experts design and theorize about. Theirs is a highly technical knowledge as well, but of a more practical nature.

— *Executives*: These are the people who make business, economic, administrative, legal, governmental, political decisions on the stuff that the experts and technicians work with. If it's a new product, they decide whether to produce and market it. If it's a new power technology, they decide whether the city should implement it. Executives are likely to have as little technical knowledge about the subject as nonspecialists.

— *Nonspecialists*: These readers have the least technical knowledge of all. Their interest may be as practical as technicians', but in a different way. They want to use the new product to accomplish their tasks; they want to understand the new power technology enough to know whether to vote for or against it in the upcoming bond election. Or, they may just be curious about a specific technical matter and want to learn about it – but for no specific, practical reason.

It's important to determine which of the four categories just discussed the potential readers of your document belong to, but that's not the end of it. Audiences, regardless of category, must also be analyzed in terms of characteristics such as the following:

— *Background-knowledge, experience, training*: One of your most important concerns is just how much knowledge, experience, or training you can expect in your readers. If you say no, then you run the risk of customers' getting frustrated with your product. If you say yes to adding background information on Windows, you increase your work effort and add to the page count of the document (and thus to the cost). Obviously, there's no easy answer to this question – part of the answer may involve just how small a segment of the audience needs that background information.

— *Needs and interests*: To plan your document, you need to know what your audience is going to expect from that document. Imagine how readers will want to use your document; what will they demand from it. For example, imagine you are writing a manual on how to use a new microwave oven – what are your readers going to expect to find in it? Imagine you're under contract to write a background report on global warming for a national real estate association – what do they want to read about; and, equally important, what do they not want to read about?

— *Other demographic characteristics*: And of course there are many other characteristics about your readers that might have an influence on how you should design and write your document – for example, age groups, type of residence, area of residence, sex, political preferences, and so on.

Audience analysis can get complicated by at least two other factors: mixed audience types for one document, wide variability within audience, and unknown audiences.

More than one audience: You're likely to find that your report is for more than one audience. For example, it may be seen by technical people (experts and technicians) and administrative people (executives). You can either write all the sections so that all the audiences of your document can understand them.

Wide variability in an audience: You may realize that, although you have an audience that fits into only one category, there is a wide variability in its background. This is a tough one – if you write to the lowest common denominator of reader, you're likely to end up with a cumbersome, tedious book-like thing that will turn off the majority of readers. But if you don't write to that lowest level, you lose that segment of your readers. Most writers go for the majority of readers and sacrifice that minority that needs more help. Others put the supplemental information in appendixes or insert cross-references to beginners' books.

Audience Adaptation

The business of writing to your audience may have a lot to do with in-born talent, intuition, and even mystery. But there are some controls you can use to have a better chance to connect with your readers. The following "controls" have mostly to do with making technical information more understandable for nonspecialist audiences:

— *Add information readers need to understand your document*: Check to see whether certain key information is missing – for example, a critical series of steps from a set of instructions; important background that helps beginners understand the main discussion; definition of key terms.

— *Omit information your readers do not need*: Unnecessary information can also confuse and frustrate readers – after all, it's there so they feel obligated to read it. For example, you can probably chop theoretical discussion from basic instructions.

— *Change the level of the information you currently have*: You may have the right information but it may be "pitched" at too high or too low a technical level. It may be pitched at the wrong kind of audience – for example, at an expert audience rather than a technician audience. This happens most often when product-design notes are passed off as instructions.

— *Add examples to help readers understand*: Examples are one of the most powerful ways to connect with audiences, particularly in instructions. Even in noninstructional text, for example, when you are trying to explain a technical concept, examples are a major help – analogies in particular.

— *Change the level of your examples*: You may be using examples but the technical content or level may not be appropriate to your readers. Homespun examples may not be useful to experts; highly technical ones may totally miss your nonspecialist readers.

— *Change the organization of your information*: Sometimes, you can have all the right information but arrange it in the wrong way. For example, there can be too much background information up front (or too little) such that certain readers get lost. Sometimes, background information needs to woven into the main information – for example, in instructions it's sometimes better to feed in chunks of background at the points where they are immediately needed.

— *Strengthen transitions*: It may be difficult for readers, particularly nonspecialists, to see the connections between the main sections of your report, between individual paragraphs, and sometimes even between individual sentences. You can make these connections much clearer by adding transition words and by echoing key words more accurately.

  Words like "therefore," "for example," "however" are transition words – they indicate the logic connecting the previous thought to the upcoming thought. You can also strengthen transitions by carefully echoing the same key words. In technical prose, it's not a good idea to vary word choice-use the same words so that people don't get any more confused than they may already be.

— *Write stronger introductions*: both for the whole document and for major sections. People seem to read with more confidence and understanding when they have the "big picture" – a view of what's coming, and how it relates to what they've just read. Therefore, make sure you have a strong introduction to the entire document – one that makes clear the topic, purpose, audience, and contents of that document. And for each major section within your document, use mini-introductions that indicate at least the topic of the section and give an overview of the subtopics to be covered in that section.

— *Create topic sentences for paragraphs and paragraph groups*: It can help readers immensely to give them an idea of the topic and purpose of a section (a group of paragraphs) and in particular to give them an overview of the subtopics about to be covered. Roadmaps help when you're in a different state.

— *Change sentence style and length*: How you write – down at the individual sentence level – can make a big difference too. In instructions, for example, using imperative voice and "you" phrasing is vastly more understandable than the passive voice or third-personal phrasing. For some reason, personalizing your writing style and making it more relaxed and informal can make it more accessible and understandable.

Passive, person-less writing is harder to read – put people and action in your writing. Similarly, go for active verbs as opposed to be verb phrasing. All of this makes your writing more direct and immediate – readers don't have to dig for it. And obviously, sentence length matters as well. An average of somewhere between 15 and 25 words per sentence is about right; sentences over 30 words are to be mistrusted.

— *Work on sentence clarity and economy*: This is closely related to the previous "control" but deserves its own spot. Often, writing style can be so wordy that it is hard or frustrating to read. When you revise your rough drafts, put them on a diet-go through a draft line by line trying to reduce the overall word, page or line count by 20 percent. Try it as an experiment and see how you do. You'll find a lot of fussy, unnecessary detail and inflated phrasing you can chop out.

— *Use more or different graphics*: For nonspecialist audiences, you may want to use more graphics – and simpler ones at that. Writing for specialists and experts tends to be less illustrated, less graphically attractive – even boring to the eye! Graphics for specialists tend to be more detailed, more technical. In technical documents for nonspecialists, there also tend to be more "decorative" graphics – ones that serve no strict informative or persuasive purpose at all.

— *Break text up or consolidate text into meaningful, usable chunks*: For nonspecialist readers, you may need to have shorter paragraphs. Notice how much longer paragraphs are in technical documents written for specialists. (Maybe a 6- to 8-line paragraph is the dividing line.)

— *Add cross-references to important information*: In technical information, you can help nonspecialist readers by pointing them to background sources. If you can't fully explain a topic on the spot, point to a book or article where it is.

— *Use headings and lists*: Readers can be intimidated by big dense paragraphs of writing, uncut by anything other than a blank line now and then. Search your rough drafts for ways to incorporate headings – look for changes in topic or subtopic. Search your writing for listings of things – these can be made into vertical lists. Look for paired listings such as terms and their definitions – these can be made into two-column lists. Of course, be careful not to force this special formatting – don't overdo it.

— *Use special typography, and work with margins, line length, line spacing, type size, and type style*: For nonspecialist readers, you can do things like making the lines shorter (bringing in the margins), using larger type sizes, and other such tactics. Certain type styles are believed to be friendlier and more readable than others.

These are the kinds of "controls" that professional technical writers use to finetune their work and make it as readily understandable as possible. And in contrast, it's the accumulation of lots of problems in these areas – even seemingly minor ones – that add up to a document being difficult to read and understand. Nonprofessionals often question why professional writers and editors insist on bothering with such seemingly picky, trivial, petty details in writing – but they all add up. It reminds me of some Chinese saying about "death by a thousand cuts."

Brainstorming

Informational Reports

A great variety of informational reports simply present information in an objective, organized way. People often need informative reports that gather and present information on a subject in one neat package. These people don't have time to do an exhaustive library search nor time to read stacks of books and articles looking for their information. Instead, they find individuals or groups to do the information gathering and report writing for them. Here are some more specific examples:

The acceptability of bikelanes in the city
The profitability of recycling municipal waste
Whether a salt water conversion facility would solve the county's fresh water problems
Whether solar energy devices will save money if installed in city-owned housing

Feasibility Reports

Recommendations, or feasibility reports as they are called here, go one step further than informational reports. They not only provide information but argue for certain courses of action (to build or not to build, to purchase or not to purchase).

Feasibility reports present information to prove whether a project can be done and whether it is worth doing. For example, a company may benefit from a new technology: but no one is sure whether the expense, the downtime, and the pay-off will be worth it.

A community may be considering a plan to build some new facility or to start some new program: but people disagree about its value or potential benefit to the community. Again, a feasibility report tries to answer these questions. Here are some more specific examples:

The acceptability of bikelanes in the city
The profitability of recycling municipal waste
Whether a salt water conversion facility would solve the county's fresh water problems
Whether solar energy devices will save money if installed in city-owned housing

Instructions

Another common use of technical writing is instructions: explanations of how to operate or repair machinery, how to perform certain actions, or what to do in certain situations. Informational-report-type information is also supplied in instructional writing: descriptions of the devices being used or explanations of principles and theory related to the activity being explained. Here are some examples of instructional topics:

How to write a metric conversion program in Pascal
How to read architectural drawings
How to develop your own photographs

How to graft a fruit tree
How to take blood pressure
How to overhaul a carburetor

To find a good report topic, let your mind wander; do some casual, relaxed browsing around. Scribble down the ideas that come to you. If you have several ideas, keep them all in mind through the early stages of your report work until one proves to be more interesting or manageable.

Major, Future Courses, and Textbooks

An obvious place to start your search is your major. On your worksheet, jot down a description of your major; include any information on special areas of interest or curiosity and on reasons you are majoring in the field. Also, list descriptions of majors or fields that you almost went into or have some interest in. On your worksheet, write any topic that comes to mind during this process.

Nursing	Business	Computer science
Data processing	Technical communications	Accounting
Biology	Financial planning	Physical education
Real estate		Elementary education
Criminology		

Take a look at your degree plan or your course catalog: what specialized courses will you be taking? Write brief descriptions of these on your worksheet, particularly ones you are looking forward to. Think about these descriptions, and scribble down any topics that come to mind. Courses or fields like these suggest a variety of technical report topics:

Management of small business	Computer graphics
Technological innovation: bioethical issues	Economics of health care
Pascal programming	Issues in nutrition and health
Business law	Urban transportation problems

Development of the young child
Criminology
Introduction to artificial intelligence
The money market
Introduction to word processing
Interior design
COBOL for business applications
Nonverbal communication

Investigate textbooks in your major, in particular, textbooks in advanced or specialized courses such as those you listed above in the section on future courses. Glance at the tables of contents of these books and at the headings. As this process begins to suggest ideas for report topics, scribble them out on your worksheet.

Instructors in your major or related fields are also good prospects for helping you find report topics. Drop by their offices for a chat; see what ideas they have. If they make interesting suggestions, jot them down. Librarians are also good prospects. Ask your librarian for a list of report subjects. Scan lists like the one below for interesting subjects. As you glance at this list, jot down the topics that interest you.

Magazines, Journals, and Periodical Indexes

Another good strategy (and an enjoyable pastime as well) for finding report topics is to do some selective browsing through magazines and journals. Check the tables of contents, and skim the titles for interesting articles in both recent and back issues. Look into magazines and journals of fields that you are curious about but may have shied away from because of their technicality. As you browse, jot down brief descriptions of possible report topics. A good way to look at a lot of magazine article titles at once is to do some selective browsing through periodical indexes.

Career plans, Interviews, and Current Work

An interesting strategy is to sit back and imagine what you'll be doing in five to ten years. Visualize the work you'll be doing or would like to be doing, and in particular, the situations that might require you to write reports. As you muse upon your future, jot down the technical subject areas you think you'll be involved in. For example:

drafting	nursing	programming
electronics	agriculture	forestry
wildlife preservation	city planning	college administration
	medicaltechnology	

Similarly, talk to business and professional people whom you know: ask them about the reports that they write or that they know about. You may end up writing a technical report for someone! And, if you currently have a job, take a look around you and see what kinds of things are going on that might require written reports. Ask:

— What reports are written or, in fact, need to be written?

— What changes or innovations are needed?

— What new equipment can be acquired to streamline the office?

— Can you propose that the business open up a new store

— somewhere else in town or in a nearby city?

Projects like these often require written reports. As these ideas occur to you, jot them down on your worksheet.

Local Improvements

Another way to find topics is to jump in the car with a friend and go driving around looking for civic projects that would make your community a better place in which to live:

— Are there esplanades or vacant areas that could be planted with trees or turned into community gardens?

— Is parking a problem in certain areas of the city?

— How is municipal garbage handled?

— Is there a recycling program in town?

— Are there bike lanes?

— Are more recreational facilities, for example, softball parks, needed?

— Are there old, unused, run-down buildings that could be renovated and used for worthwhile causes or projects?

— Would city residents be attracted to an outdoor theater for concerts, plays, and musicals?

You can also visit business people, government officials, or directors of nonprofit organizations and ask them about their needs. For example, the local senior citizens center may need barriers removed and other facilities built so that its members can get to the nearby park. For such needs, you can do the design work, calculate costs, and find out about administrative approvals that are needed. If you do your work well, the senior citizens will receive a useful report that will save them much time and effort.

Good report topics can also be found by free associating around the word "problems." Think about the problems that exist in your community, your city, your county, or your state. Think about problems geographically (as above) or socially (in terms of age, sex, race, handicaps) or in other ways (medicine, environment, politics, energy, or military). Does your field or major offer solutions, or are you interested in some of the new solutions under research? As ideas come to you, jot them down on your worksheet.

Invention

The invention stage, brainstorming what you can say about a reoport topic you have chosen. Early in your planning for a technical report, you must identify the specific audience that will read your report and the purpose your report will serve. To analyze the report audience, you must consider these questions carefully:

— Why does the audience need or want this report?

— What is the audience's technical background (knowledge, training, first-hand experience)?

— What is the report's purpose?

— What kinds of information will have to be included and excluded from the report, considering the audience?

— How should the information in the report be presented?

If you are not familiar with analyzing report audiences and purposes, return to the section where this is covered. Understanding the audience and purpose of your report becomes very important when you narrow your report subject. Briefly describe your audience, its background, capabilities, and interest in your report.

Invention Stage

Once you've picked a subject for your report, the next step is to list the topics related to it. During this stage, the "invention" or "brainstorming" stage, use the following suggestions to explore your report idea:

Let your report subject itself suggest topics: for example,

Subject	Possible topics
The sun	its temperature
	its composition
	its unusual phenomenon
	its relative size
Ultrasound in medicine	its physical properties
	equipment used
	medical uses
	advantages

— Free associate on your report subject; sit back, relax, and let your mind wander freely around the report subject. Keep scratch paper handy, however. Don't expect the ideas to come all at once in a ten-minute session: ideas for reports come at the oddest moments--in the shower, on the bus, in your backyard, in your car, or on your bicycle.

— Use an invention checklist like the following. If you ask yourself the questions listed below, you'll be less apt to overlook important topics; and, with use, these questions eventually become almost automatic.

Narrowing

No matter how fascinating your report subject is, you still must spend some time narrowing it. Narrowing a report subject means reducing it to a manageable size: something you can accomplish within a certain amount of time and within a certain number of pages.

Narrowing is like zooming in on a subject and selecting only a few topics to report on, according to your report-writing situation, specific audience, and specific purpose. Narrowing also means deciding whether to cover those topics in a general, specific, technical, or nonspecialist way. To narrow a report subject, follow these steps:

— Make as complete a list of topics related to your report subject as you can by following steps in the section "The invention or brainstorming stage."

— Look up entries on that subject in both general and specialized encyclopedias to help develop this topic list also. Encyclopedia entries are usually written in a comprehensive way; use them to build your topic list.

— When you have a sizeable list of topics related to your report subject, you are ready to do the real work of narrowing, which means asking questions like these:

- — Is this section necessary to my audience's needs?
- — Will my audience be lost and confused without this subsection?
- — Is the information included in this section crucial to my audience's understanding and to the uses to which they'll put my report?
- — Could I delete this section without harming the overall effect or purpose of my report?
- — Is the level of discussion in this section too general for my audience? too technical? not technical enough?

The audience and purpose of your report act like filters, screening out the unnecessary topics. An audience of homeowners interested in wind-powered electrical systems would want to read general information on how such systems work, what are the financial savings, and how to select a system:

- — If you are not familiar with the different audiences that reports commonly have. The steps there show you how to analyze your audience systematically and what to do if you're not sure who your audience is.
- — One last step in the narrowing process is to decide how to discuss the topics you've selected. You can discuss topics within a report in several ways:
  - — General discussion gives a rapid overview of a topic and can take up less space in a report. General discussion can be for either specialist or nonspecialist readers. In a general discussion for specialists, you save space by assuming those readers have a certain level of knowledge.
  - — Specific discussion gives much detail about a topic and thus usually takes up more space within a report. Specific discussion can also be for either specialist or nonspecialist readers. In a specific discussion for

nonspecialist readers, you make sure every detail is explained thoroughly so that those readers can understand.

Outlining

When you write a technical report, not only must you think of the right information to include (or exclude); you must also find a good way to arrange it. The first task involves invention (or brainstorming) and narrowing; the second, outlining.

Outlines for technical reports are usually hard to handle solely in your mind; it's a little like trying to add a list of large numbers in your mind. You must get report outlines on paper in order to think about the arrangement of the topics within them. A good working outline serves you in at least four important ways:

— It shows you which areas of information to investigate and gather information on.

— It shows you which areas you can safely ignore (thus saving you plenty of time).

— It enables you to schedule your work into manageable units of time.

— It gives you a "global" view of your report project, an overall sense of the contents, parts and organization of the report.

Exploratory Reading

If you have trouble getting started on the rough outline, do some exploratory reading in nonspecialist encyclopedias, introductory chapters of general audience books, or articles in science magazines for nonspecialists. If necessary, move on from these resources to more specialized ones like the McGraw-Hill Encyclopedia of Science and Technology or Van Nostrand's Scientific Encyclopedia.

Arranging Parts of Outline

If you went through the brainstorming and narrowing steps, you have a list of topics that you can rearrange into a rough outline. It will be a "rough" outline because it may still need further rearrangement and addition of other topics or subtopics. The topic list below concerns cocombustion, which is the incineration of municipal solid waste (MSW) with conventional fuels to reduce conventional fuel consumption costs and related MSW disposal problems. Imagine that you had developed a topic list on this subject and then had narrowed the list to these topics:

Advantages of cocombustion	Steps in cocombusting MSW
Disadvantages of cocombustion	Historical background on cocombustion
Economics of cocombustion	Special components for cocombustion
Composition of MSW	

The next step in outlining is to arrange the items in an appropriate order. There are so many different patterns of arrangement that only most common ones can be reviewed here.

- One of the most common patterns in outlining is the chronological one. In a historical background section of an outline, the chronological approach is just about the only one you can use.
- In some outlines, however, you almost don't notice the chronological pattern. For example, effects come after causes; solutions, after problems; or findings, after research method. The chronological pattern is most important in a research proposal outline:

I. Introduction

  A. Historical background on caffeine studies (past)

B. Objectives of the study

C. Limitations of the study

D. Plan of development

II. Review of the literature on caffeine

III. Experimental method to be used

IV. Results of the tests

V. Discussion of the results

VI. Summary and conclusions

VII. Implications for further research (future)

— Chronologically, the researcher first defines the problem, the reviews the literature on the problem, plans a research method, conducts the research and gathers data, analyzes the data and draws conclusions from it. Afterward, she may consider areas for further research on the problem.

— Another common outlining pattern is to stárt with an object at rest, motionless as if in a photograph, and then to move to a discussion of it in operation, in action as if in a motion picture.

3

Technical Reports

For many students, the technical report is the longest document they've ever written. It normally involves some research; often the information comes not only from published sources in the library, but also sources outside the library, including nonpublished things such as interviews, correspondence, and video tapes. It may also be the fanciest document: it uses binding and covers and has special elements such as a table contents, title page, and graphics.

As you think about what you want to write about for this project, don't shy away from topics you are curious about or interested in, but don't know much about. You don't need to do exhaustive research; normally, you can pull together information for an excellent report from several books and a half-dozen articles.

How well you use headings, lists, notices; how well you incorporate graphics; how well you handle the front- and back-matter elements; and how nice a job you do of turning out the final copy of the report. You don't need a fancy laser printer and you don't need to be a trained graphic artist to produce a fine-looking report. A simple typewriter or dot-matrix printer, scissors, tape, whiteout, a good-quality photocopier, and access to nice (but inexpensive) binding are all you need. Plan on doing a first-rate job on the report; remember that past students have shown prospective employers their reports and have benefited by doing so.

Your job in this unit then is define the following:

— *Report topic*: Decide what subject you are going to write on; narrow it as much as possible.

— *Report purpose*: Define what the report will accomplish—what needs of the audience it is going to fufill.

— *Report type*: Decide on the type of report—for example, technical background report, feasibility report, instructions, or some other.

You can do these in any order: for some people, it helps to start by defining an audience or a report type first. For others, beginning by picking a topic is more stimulating. Once you have defined these elements, you can start testing your report-project ideas by asking yourself these questions:

— Is there hard, specific, factual data for this topic?

— Will there be at least one or two graphics?

— Is there some realistic need for this report?

Types of Technical Reports

Technical-background report: The background report is the hardest to define but the most commonly written. This type of technical report provides background on a topic—for example, solar energy, global warming, CD-ROM technology, a medical problem, or U.S. recycling activity. However, the information on the topic is not just for anybody who might be interested in the topic, but for some individual or group that has specific needs for it and is even willing to pay for that information. For example, imagine an engineering firm bidding on a portion of the work to build a hemodialysis clinic. The engineers need to know general knowledge about renal disease and the technologies used to treat it, but they don't want to have to go digging in the library to find it. What they need is a technical background report on the subject.

Instructions: These are probably the most familiar of all the types of reports. Students often write backup procedures for the jobs they do at their work. Others write short user manuals for an appliance, equipment, or program. If there is too much to write about, they write about some smaller segment—for example, instead of instructions on using all of WordPerfect, just a guide on writing macros in WordPerfect.

Feasibility, recommendation, and evaluation reports: Another useful type of report is one that studies a problem or opportunity and then makes a recommendation. A feasibility report tells whether a project is "feasible"--that is, whether it is practical and technologically possible. A recommendation report compares two or more alternatives and recommends one (or, if necessary, none). An evaluation or assessment report studies something in terms of its worth or value For example, a college might investigate the feasibility of giving every student an e-mail address and putting many of the college functions online. The same college might also seek recommendations on the best hardware and software to use (after the feasibility report had determined it was a good idea). In practice, however, it's hard to keep these two kinds of reports distinct. Elements of the feasibility and recommendation report intermingle in specific reports--but the main thing is to get the job done!

Primary research report: Primary research refers to the actual work someone does in a laboratory or in the field--in other words, experiments and surveys. You may have written a "lab report," as they are commonly called, for one of your previous courses. This is a perfectly good possibility for the technical report as well. In this type of report, you not only present your data and draw conclusions about it, but also explain your methodology, describe the equipment and facilities you used, and give some background on the problem. You can modify this type by summarizing other primary research reports.

Technical specifications: In this report type, you discuss some new product design in terms of its construction, materials, functions, features, operation, and market potential. True specifications are not much on writing—the text is dense, fragmented; tables, lists, and graphics replace regular sentences and paragraphs whenever possible. Thus, specifications are not a good exercise of your writing abilities. However, you can write a more high-level version—one that might be read by marketing and planning executives.

Report-length proposal: As you may be aware, proposals can be monster documents of hundreds or even thousands of pages. Most of the elements are the same, just bigger. Plus elements from other kinds of reports get imported--such as feasibility discussion, review of literature, and qualifications; these become much more elaborate. The problem with writing a proposal in the technical-writing class is coordinating it with the proposal you write at the beginning of the semester. Several students have set up scenarios in which they proposed internally to write an external proposal, in which they went after some contract or grant.

Business prospectus: If you are ambitious to run your own business, you can write a business prospectus, which is a plan or proposal to start a new business or to expand an existing one. It is aimed primarily at potential investors. Therefore, it describes the proposed business, explores the marketplace and the competition, projects revenues, and describes the operation and output of the proposed business. Don't feel constrained by this list; if there is a type of technical document you want to write not listed here, talk to your instructor. It may be that we are using different names for the same thing.

A critical step in your early report planning is to define a specific audience and situation in which to write the report. For example, if you wanted to write about CD audio players, the audience cannot be this vague sort of "anybody who is considering purchasing a CD player." You have to define the audience in terms of its knowledge, background, and need for the information.

— Why does the audience need this information?

— How will readers get access to this information?

You also have to define the audience in terms of who they are specifically: that means things like names, organization or company, street address and phone numbers, and occupation or position. Just as critical to the planning process is defining the situation. When you define audience, you define who the readers are, what they know or don't know in relation to the topic, what experience or background they have in relation to the topic, and why they want or might need the information. Sometimes this leaves out a critical element: just what are the circumstances that bring about the need for the information.

Just about any topic can be worked into a good technical-report project. Some are a little more difficult than others; that's where your instructor can help. And, that is why there is the proposal assignment: it gives your instructor a chance to see what you want to do and to guide you away from problems such as the following:

Editorializing: For the report project, avoid editorial topics. For example, don't attempt to write a technical report on the pro's and con's of gun control, abortion, marijuana, and the like. You can, however, develop these topics: for example, describe the chemical, physiological aspects of marijuana or the medical techniques for abortion or the developmental stages of the fetus. These get into substantial technical areas. But avoid editorializing--there are other courses where you can do this.

Fuzzy topics: Some topics just don't work, for some reason. For example, dream analysis can be very fuzzy and nebulous. So can UFOs. You want your report to have hard factual data in it. The preceding topics are difficult to pin down this way. However, good reports have been written on the apparatus used in dream research laboratories. Maybe somebody can even figure out a good way to handle UFOs.

Tough technical topics: As mentioned earlier, don't shy away from interesting topics that you don't feel you know enough about. No one expects a doctoral thesis. Use the report project as a chance to learn something new. Of course, it's common sense that we often write better about things we know about. If this is a concern for you, look around you in your work, hobbies, or academic studies.

At the same time, however, don't be concerned that your has to be about computers, electronics, or some other "technical" topic. Remember that the word technical refers to any body of specialized knowledge.

Instructors as software: And of course if you are absolutely stumped, get with your instructor. Use your instructor as a brainstorming device. Here are some areas in which you can look for topics as well:

— *Your major, future courses*: Think about some the courses you have taken or will soon be taking within your major. Browse through some textbooks used in those courses.

— *Magazines, journals, periodical indexes*: Do some browsing in magazines and journals that are of interest to you. Indexes are a terrific way of brainstorming for a topic--they are huge lists of topics!

— *Career plans, current work*: Consider what sorts of work you will be doing in your chosen field; you may be able to think of some topics by this means. Take a look around you at work--there may be some possibilities there as well.

— *Ideas for improvements*: Take a look around your home, school, neighborhood, or city. What needs to be fixed, improved? Thinking along these lines can also lead to some good topics.

— *Problems*: Think about problems--your own, the city's, the state's, the country's, the world's. Think about problem in relation to certain groups of people. There are plenty of topics here as well.

Characteristics of Technical Reports

You're probably wondering what this technical report is supposed to look like. Ask your instructor to show you a few example reports. In addition to that, here is a brief review of some of the chief characteristics of the technical report:

— *Graphics*: The report should have graphics. Graphics include all kinds of possibilities. If you can't think of any graphics for your report project, you may not have a good topic. Get in touch with your instructor, who can help you brainstorm for graphics.

— *Factual detail*: The report should be very detailed and factual. The point of the report is to go into details, the kind of details your specific audience needs.

— *Information sources*: Your report should make use of information sources. These may include not only books and articles that can be found in libraries but also technical brochures, interviews or correspondence with experts, as well as first-hand inspections. If you don't believe any information sources are necessary for your report project, contact your instructor.

— *Documentation*: When you use borrowed information in your technical report, be sure to cite your sources. The style of citing your sources (also called "documenting" your sources) used in this course is called the number system.

— *Realistic audience and situation*: The report must be defined for a real or realistic group of readers who exist in a real or realistic situation. Most students invent an audience and situation. And the audience can't merely be something like "anybody who might be interested in global warming." Instead, it has to be real, realistic, and specific: for example, "Texas Coastal Real Estate Developers Association, interested in reliable information on global warming, to be used to aid in long-range investment planning."

— *Headings and lists*: The report should use the format for headings that is required for the course, as well as various kinds of lists as appropriate.

— *Special format*: The technical report uses a rather involved format including covers, binding, title page, table of contents, list of figures, transmittal letter, and appendixes.

— *Production*: The technical report should be typed or printed out neatly. If graphics are taped in, the whole report must be photocopied, and the photocopy handed in (not the original with the taped-in graphics). The report must be bound in some way.

— *Length*: The report should be at least 8 doublespaced typed or printed pages (using 1-inch margins), counting from introduction to conclusion. This is a minimum; a report of this length is rather skimpy. There is no real maximum length, other than what your time, energy, and stamina can handle. But remember that sheer weight does not equal quality (or better grade). If you get into a bind with a report project that would take too many pages, contact your instructorthere are numerous tricks we can use to cut it down to size.

— *Technical content*: You must design your report project in such a way that your poor technical-writing instructor has a chance to understand it--in other words, you must write for the nonspecialist. Also, at some point, you may get concerned about the technical accuracy of your information. Remember that this is a writing course, not a course in engineering, nursing, science, electronics, or the like. Make a good-faith effort to get the facts right, but don't go overboard.

Other Types of Technical Reports

For the final report, you can write one of (or even a combination) of several different types of reports. These choices are not meant to be restrictive, but to indicate a range of possibilities. If there is some other type of report that you know about and want to write, get with your instructor to discuss it.

Organizational policies and procedures: These are the operating documents for organizations; they contain rules and regulations on how the organization and its members are expected to perform. Policies and procedures are like instructions, but they go much further.

Feasibility, evaluation, recommendation reports. This group of similar reports does things like compare several options against a set of requirements and recommend one; considers an idea (plan, project) in terms of its "feasibility," in terms of some combination of its technical, economical, social practicality or possibility; passes judgement on the worth or value of a thing by comparing it to a set of requirements, or criteria.

Technical background reports: This type is the hardest one to define but the one that most people write. It focuses on a technical topic, provides a certain background on that topic for a specific set of readers who have specific needs for it.

Primary research reports: This type presents findings and interpretation from laboratory or field research.

Technical Background Reports

The technical background report is hard to define—it's not a lot of things, but it's hard to say what it is. It doesn't provide step-by-step directions on how to do something the way that instructions do. It does not formally provide recommendations the way that feasibility reports do. It does not report data from original research and draw conclusions the way that primary research reports do. So what does the technical background report do? It provides information on a technical topic but in such a way that is adapted for a particular audience that has specific needs for that information. Imagine a topic like this: renal disease and therapy.

A technical background report on this topic would not dump out a ten-ton textbook containing everything you could possibly say about it. It would select information about the topic suited to a specific group of readers who had specific needs and uses for the information. Imagine the audience was a group of engineers bidding on a contract to do part of the work for a dialysis clinic. Yes, they need to know about renal disease and its therapy, but only to the extent that it has to do with their areas of expertise. Such a background report might also include some basic discussion of renal disease and its treatment, but no more than what the engineers need to do their work and to interact with representatives of the clinic.

Take a look at an example of a technical background report, starting on page. This one is an exploration of global warming, or the greenhouse effect, as it is called in the report. Notice that it discusses causes, then explores the effects, then discusses what can be done about it. Typical contents and organization of technical background reports.

Because it focuses on a specific technical topic for specific audiences who have specific needs or uses for the information, it grabs at whatever type of contents it needs to get the job done. You use a lot of intuition to plan this type of report. For example, with the report on renal disease and treatment, you'd probably want to discuss what renal disease is, what causes it, how it is treated, and what kinds of technologies are involved in the treatment. If you don't fully trust your intuition, use a checklist like the following:

— *Definitions*: a checklist like the following -Define the potentially unfamiliar terms associated with the topic. Write extended definitions if the terms are key terms or if they are particularly difficult to explain.

— *Causes*: Explain what causes are related to the topic. For example, with the renal disease topic, what causes the disease?

— *Effects*: Explain what are the consequences, results, or effects associated with the topic. With the renal disease topic, what happens to people with the disease; what effects do the various treatments have?

— *Types*: Discuss the different types or categories associated with the topic. For example, are there different types of renal disease; are there different categories of treatment?

— *Historical background*: Discuss relevant history related to the topic. Discuss people, events, and past theories related to the topic.

— *Processes*: Discuss mechanical, natural, human-controlled processes related to the topic. Explain step by step how the process occurs. For example, what are the phases of the renal disease cycle; what typically happens to a person with a specific form of the disease?

— *Descriptions*: Provide information on the physical details of things related to the topic. Provide information about size, shape, color, weight, and so on.

— *Comparisons*: Compare the topic, or some aspect of it, to something similar or something familiar. With the renal disease example, you could compare renal disease to some other disease; the treatment to some treatment; the functions of the kidney to something familiar (an analogy); or even the treatment to something familiar, for example, the filter system for a swimming pool.

— *Applications*: Explore how some aspect of your topic can be used or applied. If it's some new technology, what are its applications?

— *Advantages and disadvantages*: Discuss the advantages or disadvantages of one or more aspects of your topic. In the renal disease topic, for example, what are the advantages of one treatment over another?

— *Economic considerations*: Discuss the costs of one or more aspects associated with your topic. How much does treatment for renal disease cost? How much does the equipment and personnel cost?

— *Social, political, legal, ethical implications*: Explore the implications or impact of your topic or some aspect of it in relation to social, political, legal, or ethical concerns. The renal disease example doesn't lend itself much to this area, but imagine the possibilities with a topic like cryogenics—suspended animation of human beings. Often, new technologies have profound impact in these areas.

— *Problems, questions*: What problems or questions are there associated with your report topic or some aspect of it?

— *Solutions, answers*: What solutions or answers can you offer on those problems or questions raised by your topic or some aspect of it?

Primary Research Reports

Primary research report is a report that presents original research data--no matter whether that data was generated in a laboratory or out in the "field." A secondary research report then would be a report that presents information gained largely from printed information sources or from other sources such as people. You're probably already familiar with this type of report as the "lab report." The contents and organization of this type of report have a basic logic: you present your data and conclusions, but also present information on how you went about the experiment or survey. In other words, you enable the reader to replicate (the fancy scientific word for repeat) your experiment, or at least, visualize quite specifically how you went about it.

Typical contents of primary research reports. To enable readers to replicate your e::periment or survey, you provide information like the following:

— *Introduction* :The introduction to the primary research report needs to do what any good introduction to a report needs to do--get the readers ready to read the report. It may provide some background, but not more than a paragraph or two in a one- to two-page introduction. Some of the common elements of the introduction to a primary research report, such as the background or the purpose, can be handled in the introduction. If they require a lot of discussion, however, they may need their own sections.

— *Problem, background*: One of the first things to do, either in the introduction, or in a separate section of its own, is to discuss the situation that has led to the research work. For example, you may find that there is something questionable about a commonly accepted theory; you may have noticed some phenomenon that could be used to advantage, and so on. Explain this somewhere toward the beginning of a primary research report.

— *Purpose, objectives, scope*: Also toward the beginning of this type of report discuss what you intended to do in the research project--what were your objectives? Also, explain the scope of your work—what were you not trying to do?

— *Review of literature*: After you've established the basis for the project, summarize the literature relevant to it--for example, books, journal articles, and encyclopedias. If you are doing a study on grammar-checking software, what books or articles have already been written on that subject? What do they have to say about the merits of this kind of software? All you do is summarize this literature briefly and enable readers to go have a look at it by providing the full bibliographic citation at the end of your report.

— *Materials, equipment, facilities*: Remember that one of your goals in writing this type of report is to enable the reader to replicate the experiment or survey you performed. Key to this is the discussion of the equipment and facilities you used in your research. Describe things in detail, providing brand names, model numbers, sizes, and other such specifications.

— *Theory, methods, procedures*: To enable readers to replicate your project, you must also explain the procedures or methods you used. This discussion can be step by step: "first, I did this, then I did that...." Theory and method refer more to the intellectual or conceptual framework of your project. These explain why you used the procedures that you used.

— *Results, findings, data*: Critical to any primary research report is the data that you collect. You present it in various tables, charts, and graph. These can go in the body of your report, or in appendixes if they are so big that they interrupt the flow of your discussion. Of course, some results or findings may not be presentable as tables, charts, or graphs. In these cases, you just discuss it in paragraphs. In any case, you do not add interpretation to this presentation of data. You merely present the data, without trying to explain it.

— *Discussion, conclusions, recommendations*: In primary research reports, you interpret or discuss your findings in a section separate from the one where you present the data. Now's the time to explain your data, to interpret it. This section, or area of the report, is also the place to make recommendations or state ideas for further research.

— *Bibliography*: The ideal of the primary research report is build upon or add to the knowledge in a particular area. It's the vehicle by which our knowledge advances for a specific topic. Your primary research report rests on top of all the work done by other researchers on the same topic. For that reason, you must list the sources of information you used or consulted in your project. This list occurs at the end of the report.

As for the organization of a primary research report, the typical contents just listed are arranged in an actual primary research report in just about the same order they were just discussed. Loosely, it is a chronological order. First, you discuss set-up issues such as the problem and objectives, then you discuss the procedures, then the data resulting from those procedures, then your conclusions based upon that data. This type of report varies greatly in terms of how long the typical sections are, whether they get combined with other sections, and what they are called (their headings).

4

Business Correspondence

Mechanical and physical details of business letters are described below.

Heading: The heading contains the writer's address and the date of the letter. The writer's name is not included and only a date is needed in headings on letterhead stationery.

Inside address: The inside address shows the name and address of the recipient of the letter. This information helps prevent confusion. Also, if the recipient has moved, the inside address helps to determine what to do with the letter. In the inside address, include the appropriate title of respect of the recipient; and copy the name of the company exactly as that company writes it. When you do have the names of individuals, remember to address them appropriately: Mrs., Ms., Mr., Dr., and so on. If you are not sure what is correct for an individual, try to find out how that individual signs letters or consult the forms-of-address section in a dictionary.

Salutation: The salutation directly addresses the recipient of the letter and is followed by a colon (except when a friendly, familiar, sociable tone is intended, in which case a comma is used). Notice that in the simplified letter format, the salutation line is eliminated altogether. If you don't know whether the recipient is a man or woman, the traditional practice has been to write "Dear Sir" or "Dear

Sirs" - but that's sexist! To avoid this problem, salutations such as "Dear Sir or Madame," "Dear Ladies and Gentlemen," "Dear Friends," or "Dear People" have been tried - but without much general acceptance. Deleting the salutation line altogether or inserting "To Whom It May Concern" in its place, is not ordinarily a good solution either - it's impersonal.

The best solution is to make a quick, anonymous phone call to the organization and ask for a name; Or, address the salutation to a department name, committee name, or a position name: "Dear Personnel Department," "Dear Recruitment Committee," "Dear Chairperson," "Dear Director of Financial Aid," for example.

Subject or reference line: As shown in the order letter, the subject line replaces the salutation or is included with it. The subject line announces the main business of the letter.

Body of the letter: The actual message of course is contained in the body of the letter, the paragraphs between the salutation and the complimentary close. Strategies for writing the body of the letter are discussed in the section on business-correspondence style.

Complimentary close: The "Sincerely yours" element of the business letter is called the complimentary close. Other common ones are "Sincerely yours," "Cordially," "Respectfully," or "Respectfully yours." You can design your own, but be careful not to create florid or wordy ones. Notice that only the first letter is capitalized, and it is always followed by a comma.

Signature block: Usually, you type your name four lines below the complimentary close, and sign your name in between. If you are a woman and want to make your marital status clear, use Miss, Ms., or Mrs. in parentheses before the typed version of your first name. Whenever possible, include your title or the name of the position you hold just below your name. For example, "Technical writing student," "Sophomore data processing major," or "Tarrant County Community College Student" are perfectly acceptable.

End notations: Just below the signature block are often several abbreviations or phrases that have important functions.

Enclosures: To make sure that the recipient knows that items accompany the letter in the same envelope, use such indications as "Enclosure," "Encl.," "Enclosures." For example, if you send a resume and writing sample with your application letter, you'd do this: "Encl.: Resume and Writing Sample." If the enclosure is lost, the recipient will know.

Copies: If you send copies of a letter to others, indicate this fact among the end notations also. If, for example, you were upset by a local merchant's handling of your repair problems and were sending a copy of your letter to the Better Business Bureau, you'd write this: "cc: Better Business Bureau." If you plan to send a copy to your lawyer, write something like this: "cc: Mr. Raymond Mason, Attorney."

Following pages: If your letter is longer than one page, the heading at the top of subsequent pages can be handled in one of the following ways: If you use letterhead stationery, remember not to use it for subsequent pages. However, you must use blank paper of the same quality, weight, and texture as the letterhead paper (usually, letterhead stationery comes with matching blank paper).

Business Letter Formats

If you are writing a business letter, select one of the common formats as shown in the example letters listed below. These include the block letter, the semi-block letter, the alternative block letter, and the simplified letter.

— See the block letter.

— See the semi-block letter.

— See the alternative block letter.

— For the simplified letter.

Which of these formats to use depends on the ones commonly used in your organization or the situation in which you are writing. Use the simplified letter if you lack the name of an individual or department to write to.

Style in Business Correspondence

Writing business letters and memos differs in certain important ways from writing reports. Keep the following advice in mind when you write and especially when you revise your business letters or memos. State the main business, purpose, or subject matter right away. Let the reader know from the very first sentence what your letter is about. Remember that when business people open a letter, their first concern is to know what the letter is about, what its purpose is, and why they must spend their time reading it. Therefore, avoid round-about beginnings.

If you are writing to apply for a job, begin with something like this: "I am writing to apply for the position you currently have open...." If you have bad news for someone, you need not spill all of it in the first sentence. Here is an example of how to avoid negative phrasing: "I am writing in response to your letter of July 24, 1997 in which you discuss problems you have had with an electronic spreadsheet purchased from our company."

If you are responding to a letter, identify that letter by its subject and date in the first paragraph or sentence. Busy recipients who write many letters themselves may not remember their letters to you. Keep the paragraphs of most business letters short. The paragraphs of business letters tend to be short, some only a sentence long. Business letters are not read the same way as articles, reports, or books. Usually, they are read rapidly. Big, thick, dense paragraphs over ten lines, which require much concentration, may not be read carefully - or read at all.

To enable the recipient to read your letters more rapidly and to comprehend and remember the important facts or ideas, create relatively short paragraphs of between three and eight lines long. In business letters, paragraphs that are made up of only a single sentence are common and perfectly acceptable.

"Compartmentalize" the contents of your letter. When you "compartmentalize" the contents of a business letter, you place each different segment of the discussion - each different topic of the letter - in its own paragraph. If you were writing a complaint letter concerning problems with the system unit of your personal computer, you might have these paragraphs:

— A description of the problems you've had with it

— The ineffective repair jobs you've had

— The compensation you think you deserve and why

Study each paragraph of your letters for its purpose, content, or function. When you locate a paragraph that does more than one thing, consider splitting it into two paragraphs. If you discover two short separate paragraphs that do the same thing, consider joining them into one. Provide topic indicators at the beginning of paragraphs.

In the first sentence of any body paragraph of a business letter, try to locate a word or phrase that indicates the topic of that paragraph. If a paragraph discusses your problems with a personal computer, work the word "problems" or the phrase "problems with my personal computer" into the first sentence. Doing this gives recipients a clear sense of the content and purpose of each paragraph.

List or itemize whenever possible in a business letter. Listing spreads out the text of the letter, making it easier to pick up the important points rapidly. Place important information strategically in business letters. Information in the first and last lines of paragraphs tends to be read and remembered better. Information buried in the middle of long paragraphs is easily overlooked or forgotten.

Therefore, place important information in high-visibility points. For example, in application letters which must convince potential employers that you are right for a job, locate information on appealing qualities at the beginning or end of paragraphs for greater emphasis. Place less positive or detrimental information in less highly visible points in your business letters. If you have some difficult things to say, a good (and honest) strategy is to de-emphasize by placing them in areas of less emphasis. If a job requires three years of experience and you only have one, bury this fact in the middle or the lower half of a body paragraph of the application letter. The resulting letter will be honest and complete; it just won't emphasize weak points unnecessarily.

Find positive ways to express bad news in your business letters. Often, business letters must convey bad news: a broken computer keyboard cannot be replaced, or an individual cannot be hired. Such bad news can be conveyed in a tactful way. Doing so reduces the chances that business relations with the recipient of the bad news will end. To convey bad news positively, avoid such words as "cannot," "forbid," "fail," "impossible," "refuse," "prohibit," "restrict," and "deny" as much as possible.

Focus on the recipient's needs, purposes, or interests instead of your own. Avoid a self-centered focusing on your own concerns rather than those of the recipient. Even if you must talk about yourself in a business letter a great deal, do so in a way that relates your concerns to those of the recipient. This recipient-oriented style is often called the "you-attitude," which does not mean using more you's but making the recipient the main focus of the letter. Avoid pompous, inflated, legal-sounding phrasing. Watch out for puffed-up, important-sounding language. This kind of language may seem business-like at first; it's actually ridiculous. Of course, such phrasing is apparently necessary in legal documents; but why use it in other writing situations? When you write a business letter, picture yourself as a plain-talking, common-sense, down-to-earth person (but avoid slang).

Give your business letter an "action ending" whenever appropriate. An "action-ending" makes clear what the writer of the letter expects the recipient to do and when. Ineffective conclusions to business letters often end with rather limp, noncommittal statements such as "Hope to hear from you soon" or "Let me know if I can be of any further assistance." Instead, or in addition, specify the action the recipient should take and the schedule for that action. If, for example, you are writing a query letter, ask the editor politely to let you know of his decision if at all possible in a month. If you are writing an application letter, subtlely try to set up a date and time for an interview.

Business Plans

A business plan is very much like a proposal, except for at least one big difference. The prospectus seeks to start a new business or significantly expand an existing business. A proposal, on the other hand, seeks approval to do a specific project. For example, a business plan might seek funding and other support to start a software company to create computer games. A proposal, on the other hand, might bid to do the development work for some specific computer game. After you've read the following introductory material, refer to the special resources page for in-depth discussion of business plans.

Many of the elements of the plans resemble those of the proposal—particularly the qualifications and background sections. Remember that these sections are only typical and not necessarily in any required order. For your plan, you'll need to think about the best sequencing of the sections and about other sections that might also be necessary.

- *Product or service to be offered*: One of the most important sections of the business plan is the description of the actual product or service to be offered by your company. If it is a description of a product—a physical object—you need to use the techniques for technical description. If you are going to offer a service, explain it, and take readers on a step-by-step tour of how the service will be handled.
- *Technical background on the product or service*: If your product or service involves technologies or technical processes potentially unfamiliar to your readers, explain these. Remember that business plans often go to nonspecialists who, despite their lack of technical expertise, have the investment funds or the legal understanding to get your business going.
- *Market for the product or service*: ritical also to any business plan is the exploration of the existing marketplace into which your product or service fits. What other companies exist that offer the same thing you plan to offer? How much business do they do? How are they different from each other? How will your business differ from them?
- *Process by which the product or service is produced*: If applicable, explain how the product or service will be produced. Explain how the proposed business will operate on a day-to-day basis.
- *Facilities and personnel needed for the operation*: Plan to discuss the facilities (storefronts, warehouses, production facilities, vehicles) your business will require as well as the personnel that will be needed.
- *Projected revenues from the operation*: Of obvious importance in any business plan is the discussion of the revenues you project for your business. If you know the

estimate of total revenues for the market area in which you plan to operate, what percentage do you explain to win? Obviously, in your first few years, you may operate at a loss—at what point in time do you project to break even?

— *Funding necessary for startup and operation*: The plan should also discuss the funding you'll need to get the business started as well as the operating costs—the funding needed to run the business on a daily basis.

— *Legal issues related to the proposed business*: Your business plan may also need to discuss your business, its products, or its services in relation to government regulations—for example, environmental restrictions.

— *Qualifications and background of the personnel*: Important too is the section that presents your qualifications to start and operate the business you are proposing. Of course, "you" can mean a number of people with whom you are working to start the business.

— *Discussion of feasibility and investment potential*: You'll want to include in your plan a discussion of the likelihood of the success of your business. Obviously, you believe that it will be a success, but you must find a way to support this belief with facts and conclusions in order to convince your readers. Also, you must discuss what sort of return on investment readers can expect.

— *Investment offering*: And finally, you may need to present what kinds of investment apparatus you are actually offering.

In planning your business plan, remember that you try to provide whatever information the audience may need to consider your idea. Your goal is to convince them you have a good idea and to encourage them to invest in it (or to approve it in some way). It's okay to provide marginal information—information you're not quite sure that readers will want. After all, you section off the parts of a business plan with headings; readers can skip over sections they are not interested in.

Format for business plans

You can use the format for the formal report, the format for proposals, or some combination of the two. Business plans, even those for small operations, can run well over 15 pages—in which case you'll want to bind the plan. You'll also need a cover letter—examples of this are also in the section on report formatting. As you plan the format of your business plan, you'll want to think about designing it so that readers can find and read essential information quickly. This means setting up an abstract, but calling it "Executive Summary" or "Prospectus Overview."

Also plan to group similar sections. In the preceding section that lists the various kinds of information to include in a plan, some of suggestions should be combined—for example, the sections on financial aspects of the proposed business. And finally, make use of appendixes for unwieldy, bulky information. Enable readers to quickly find the main sections of the plan, without having to wade through tables and charts that go on for pages and pages. After you've read the preceding introductory material, refer to the special resources page for in-depth discussion of business plans.

Technical Specifications

Specifications are descriptions of products or product requirements. More broadly, they can provide details for the design, manufacture, testing, installation, and use of a product. You typically see specifications in the documentation that comes in the package with certain kinds of products, for example, CD players or computers. These describe the key technical characteristics of the item.

But specifications are also written as a way of "specifying" the construction and operational characteristics of a thing. They are then used by people who actually construct the thing or go out and attempt to purchase it. When you write specifications, accuracy, precision of detail, and clarity are critical. Poorly written specifications can cause a range of problems and lead to lawsuits.

Specifications have a particular style, format, and organization.

— Make every effort to find out what the specific requirements are for format, style, contents, and organization. If they are not documented, collect a big pile specifications written by or for your company, and study them for characteristics like thse described in the following.

— Use two-column lists or tables to lists specific details. If the purpose is to indicate details such as dimensions, materials, weight, tolerances, and frequencies, regular paragraph-style writing may be unnecessary.

— Use the decimal numbering system for each individual specification. This facilitates cross-referencing.

— Use either the open (performance) style or the closed restrictive style, depending on the requirements of the job. In the open or performance style, you can specify what the product or component should do, that is, its performance capabilities. In the closed style, you specify exactly what it should be or consist of.

— Cross-reference existing specifications whenever possible. Various goverment agencies as well as trade and professional associations publish specifications standards. You can refer to these standards rather than include the actual specifications details.

— Use specific, concrete language that identifies as precisely as possible what the product or component should be or do. Avoid words that are ambiguous--words that can be interpreted in more than one way. Use technical jargon the way it is used in the trade or profession.

— Test your specifications by putting yourself in the role of a bumbling contractor--or even an unscrupulous one. What are the ways a careless or incompetent individual could misread your specifications? Could someone willfully misread your specifications in order to cut cost, time, and quality? Obviously, no set of specifications can ultimately be "foolproof" or "shark-proof," but you must try to make them as clear and unambiguous as possible.

— For specifications to be used in design, manufacturing, construction, or procurement, use "shall" to indicate requirements. In specifications writing, "shall" is understood as indicating a requirement.

— Provide numerical specifications in both words and symbols: for example, "the distance between the two components shall be three centimeters (3 cm)."

— Writing style in specifications can be very terse: incomplete sentences are acceptable as well as the omission of functions words such as articles and conjunctions that are understood.

— Exercise great caution with pronouns and relational or qualifying phrases. Make sure there is no doubt about words such as "it," "they," "which," and "that" refer to. Watch out for sentences containing a list of two or more items followed by some descriptive phrase—does the descriptive phrase refer to all the list items or just one? In cases like these, you may have to take a wordier approach for the sake of clarity.

— Use words and phrasing that have become standard in similar specifications over the years. Past usage has proven them reliable. Avoid words and phrases that are known not to hold up in lawsuits.

— Make sure your specifications are complete—put yourself in the place of those who need your specifications; make sure you cover everything they will need.

Organization is critical in specifications—readers need to be able to find one or a collection of specific details. To facilitate the process of locating individual specifications, use headings, lists, tables, and identifying numbers as discussed previously. But a certain organization of the actual contents is also standard.

— *General description*: Describe the product, component, or program first in general terms--administrative details about its cost, start and completion dates, overall description of the project, scope of the specifications (what you are not covering), anything that is of a general nature and does not fit in the part-by-part descriptions in the following.

— *Part-by-part description*: In the main body, present specifications part by part, element by element, trade by trade--whatever is the logical, natural, or conventional way of doing it.

— *General-to-specific order*: Wherever applicable, arrange specifications from general to specific.

Use of Graphics

In specifications, use graphics wherever they enable you to convey information more effectively. For example, in the specifications for a cleanroom for production of integrated circuits, drawings, diagrams, and schematics convey some of the information much more succinctly and effectively than sentences and paragraphs.

Writing Business Plans

A business plan is a document used to start a new business or get funding for a business that is changing in some significant way. Business plans are important documents for business partners who need to agree upon and document their plans, government officials who may need to approve aspects of the plan, and of course potential investors such as banks or private individuals who may decide to fund the business or its expansion.

A business plan is obviously an important application of writing and one that may contain substantial technical information about the business operations or products. That's why it's a good option for the final project in a technical- writing course. You can write a business plan if you actually are trying to start a business or if you'd merely like to do some constructive daydreaming about a business you'd like to start. Business plans can be very large documents containing information that you may have no way of getting. Work with your instructor to reach an agreement on the scope of the business plan you write. Remember too that your instructor is probably not a professional business-startup consultant and probably won't be able to help you on the finer points of planning a business.

5

Writing of White Paper

A white paper is a government report outlining policy or authoritative report on a major issue. White papers are an effective medium that educate and inform and, most importantly, influence a prospective customer. It is considered to be a standard marketing tool today. Statistics show that decision makers in organizations use them as their first external source of information. A white paper from a company should reinforce why the organization needs to be selected over the competition.

In Commonwealth countries, it is the informal name for a parliamentary paper. In the United Kingdom they are (normally a "Command paper") issued by the government and laying out its policy, or proposed policy, on a topic of current concern. Although a white paper may occasion consultation as to the details of new legislation, it does signify a clear intention on the part of a government to pass new law. By contrast, green papers, which are issued less frequently, are more open-ended and may merely propose a strategy to be implemented in the details of other legislation. Over time, white papers have come to refer to documents that argue non-governmental positions as well. For example, many white papers today espouse the benefits of particular technologies and products.

White papers discuss a specific business issue, product, or competitive situation. In many cases, they summarize information about a topic, for example the results of a survey or study and then suggest a 'proposal for action', with the research data providing the justification for the action. In the IT industry, white paper is often produced in tandem with case studies, as they are both ultimately used as sales collateral. White papers, it's important to note, are not technical documents.

Purpose of White Papers

From one perspective, their purpose is to share technical knowledge and business information with others in the same field; for example, CIOs who are interested in how web services can be used with Ecommerce applications. They are also used as collateral material for presentations at industry conferences, promotional drives, seminars and other such events. From a business viewpoint, a white paper is used to generate publicity, especially when a company is starting out and trying to get media attention.

If a company is working on an innovative area or solutions for a specialized audience, these white papers can be very effective in demonstrating the company's achievements. It is worth noting that the main difference between an IT white paper and, for example, an academic research paper is that the IT company's writing will tend to be more guarded-so that competitors don't learn too much and steal their ideas. The writing style of white papers tends to be formal, direct, and business-like. However, they tend to avoid 'marketese'-that unique brand of marketing writing that makes outrageous product statements and comes with over-the-top claims to greatness.

Sales and Marketing

White papers are also used to support the sales strategy, in particular, when introducing a new product. It also provides valuable collateral material for the Sales and Marketing team when they are meeting clients. It is something they can leave with the client who can refer to it at their own leisure. Sales focused white papers tend to include:

1. Market analysis: this will discuss potential buyers; the most important business drivers; typical customers broken out by demographics, regions, sectors etc; and abstracts from leading market research companies that support the solution in the white paper.

2. Implementations of the product/solution supported by quotes from the client. This section details the client's business objectives, technical obstacles, the solution that was implemented and how it benefited the company.

3. Product analysis: this includes tables, charts, and graphs about the solution. All the technical specifications are distilled down to a few pages in an easy-to-read format.

4. USP- details of the Unique Selling Points supported with persuasive arguments that differentiate it from the competition.

Define the target audience/market and the purpose of the white paper, i.e., whether it is to establish authority on a particular topic, or create awareness of an upcoming issue or trend, or to provide information that will help buyers make decisions and differentiate the company from the competition. Define the message the white paper is going to deliver and ask yourself the reason why anyone would want to read it.

A White Paper usually contain

1. Current industry problems/trends: Begin with a description of the broadest issues and trends in the industry that will introduce the reader to the topic. Then move on to discussing the specific attributes of the solution.

2. Technology: Description of the technology if necessary.
3. How the service offered or the new technology or business model works.
4. Benefits/application/ROI/case studies.
5. Visual appeal: Add graphics, charts and images to break the monotony of reading text and also tools to understand the topic better.
6. How to choose a solution/vendor if applicable.
7. Summary.

White Paper Don'ts:

1. Avoid using technical acronyms and other difficult terminology.
2. Avoid technical complexity.
3. Avoid writing a user manual.

Training guidelines for a business article:

— Preparation

— Writing Plan

— Writing Process

— Promotional Copy

— Links to Business Sites

— Dictionaries, Style Manuals, Grammar Handbooks, Editing Resources

The writing process includes:

1. Writing Plan
2. Writing process:
   — Research
   — Search engine tips
3. Pre-writing

— Brainstorm

— Free writing

4. Structure of ideas and writing patterns
5. Paragraph sequence formation
6. Introduction and Conclusion ideas
7. Formatting
8. Editing
9. Rewriting

Preparation

Know thy target audience: an irrefragable rule of web writing! The article you write may supply information to the reader, help him make a decision or recommend a procedure. How much your reader knows will determine what kind of background information you need to provide.

Writing Plan

What are the skills required of a writer? Determination, patience and practice! Researching, writing, reviewing and rewriting, rewriting and rewriting!

Getting ideas: Original ideas and unusual approaches come from random thinking -- a mix of random and logical thoughts. This is a left-brain and a right brain effort.

Research: How do you research the content of your article? In some cases, what you want is easy to find. But, while writing about new trends and new ideas it is likely that you will find information in the most unlikely places.

Personal contacts and friends, your past experiences, printed information, the Internet, visual sources and companies and organizations are the various sources that can form a germinating ground for your research.

Writing Process

Collating all the information that you have so painstakingly collected and incorporating it in a writing process is what you will do next. At this stage you have not worked out the "how" of the article. You can put down whatever thoughts come to mind in a point-form without worrying about grammar and style, or even punctuation used. There are many ways of doing this, either by free writing, clustering or even using a flow chart to sequence your points. You need to form ideas at this stage, group them and then later decide on the structure and sequence of your writing.

Brainstorm: Brainstorming is a method of generating ideas using free association. All minds, however uncreative (supposedly) are wonderful tools for developing ideas and brainstorming is a sure fire way to get those itsy bitsy gems of thought out in the open.

Free writing is a fine method of developing critical thinking skills. What it means is writing free of constraints — without worrying about grammar, spelling, the right words or punctuation. Writing whatever comes to mind continuously without worrying about the style and instead concentrating on investing ideas onto a paper is the main objective here.

Mind mapping: Sketching out ideas in the form of visuals or doodles (that make some kind of sense) on a piece of paper and grouping them in clusters is a fun approach to your idea germination. We could call it the graffiti approach. What you would do here is to write a word that you associate with your topic, lets say, "search engines." Write down words related to this — keywords, descriptions etc. Now, jot down sub categories for each of these words and then group them in a logical manner. Here, you are using both the creative and logical mind (we assume that you have both). Using a colored pen you can draw lines between groups or clusters and write down the association and other ideas that occur to you.

Don't forget to jot down introductory/summary remarks, abbreviations, important facts, dates, graphs and drawings. Any personal comments you want to make regarding your article or otherwise can be bracketed.

If you are persuasively trying to sell a product or a service, you will paint a scenario that requires your product or service and then move on to describing the problems or reasons for using the product. This outline will comprise a description of the product benefits and also demolish reasons against the product. At the end, you may summarize the benefits of the product or service and then conclude in an action statement. An action statement is one that makes readers act.

The scientific form or a technical article has a framework as follows: Description of the purpose of the report or the investigation followed by the methods used in supporting this investigation, the data used and the final conclusion of your report. Using visual tools and aids here give more clarity to your findings or explanations.

Introduction to the Article

This may be the most difficult place to start. Opening remarks are crucial, even more so in web writing. A useful model to follow in the introduction is AIDA

A - Gain Attention

I - Attract Interest

D - Create Desire (Anxiety)

A - Stimulate Action

Adopt a journalistic approach or the "inverted pyramid" method. The inverted pyramid style works best here. Who, what, where, when, why and how of the information that you are going to provide summarized in gist and then the rest of the article upholding these statements is what is called the inverted pyramid approach. So, start with a conclusion and spend the rest of the essay supporting it.

Asking a question, stating an important fact, quoting someone famous, making an interesting and startling observation are some of the many ways that one can introduce a topic. The aim here is to grab the attention of the reader, a hook that seduces.

Just in case this BRILLIANT INTRODUCTION doesn't happen immediately, you can always write, "Brilliant introduction goes here," and work on it later. Complete your draft and review the points that you made. Analyzing your draft will give you an idea of the structure and the form that your article is going to take. Think of metaphors, analogies and parables or examples or any visual aids and illustrations that you can use to help the reader understand the article better.

At this juncture, you can decide which idea goes into what paragraph and the sequence of these paragraphs. Now you need to work on those individual paragraphs and, of course, write. Sentences and paragraphs begin to appear with more clarity here.

Keep in mind the following:

Organization: The opening words of a sentence convey the main idea of the sentence. The main idea of the paragraph is conveyed in the first sentence, also called the topic sentence. Don't include more than one idea to a paragraph. Vary the sentence length and pattern (about 7 to 20 words per sentence). Paragraph lengths can vary from 6 to 8 lines with appropriately titled sub-headings. Bulleted lists and adequate amount of white space aid readers who skim through articles in deciding whether the article is worth more than a cursory perusal. So, make your article pretty and easy to read.

Language: Adopt a conversational tone and use terms that your readers can picture. Don't write in the third person, you don't want your article to sound like boring official memos, do you? Put people in your writing; write to one person, use anecdotes, eyewitness accounts and other interesting fables or examples to captivate the hurried reader. Be assertive and forthright in whatever you want to say.

Eliminate non-motivating phrases and sexist language. Instead of writing "We hope to have covered all salient features in this article," accent the positive and motivate your readers with "Now, that we have covered the salient features of...." Conveying an image of confidence and credibility takes priority when writing an article. Backing up all assertions made with solid foolproof explanations comes next.

Keep your prose short and trim. Flowery language doesn't help in keeping readers on your site. The dictionary has a billion words but it does not mean that you use all of them in your article. Clean up the dead wood and use phrases and words that a reader easily understands. Immediate gratification is what most readers today are looking for.

Following things to be avoidde:

1. *Spelling and grammatical errors*: Use the spell checker on your computer and then get a peer or a friend to edit your article.
2. *Long verbs*: use shorter verbs like introduce, begin, start or commence instead of "in the beginning."
3. *Passive voice*: Eliminate sluggish passive voice expressions. Example: We need a cover letter for the final report. Instead of For the final report a cover letter was needed.
4. Use verbs of action: I received a copy. Instead of I was given a copy.

5. Not capitalizing abbreviations: Always capitalize abbreviations and expand them when you introduce them in the essay.
6. Avoid using qualifiers like little, rather and very.
7. Abstract language: Use precise language and write in the active voice.
8. Use the comma correctly.
9. Avoid wordiness: Wordiness is using lengthy words and sentences when the same idea can actually be conveyed in a more concise manner.
10. Unclear words and sentences: Don't use unfamiliar words, clichés and redundant language.

Conclusion: It usually helps to recapitulate what was said in the thesis statement. This tells your reader that you have accomplished what you set out to. You can summarize your essay, call the readers to act or suggest results or consequences.

Style: Develop an individual style of your own by writing about anything that interests you as often as you can. A useful checklist at the end of writing:

1. A powerful introduction
2. Emphasize key points in an unusual manner
3. Adopt a conversational style
4. Examples, anecdotes, illustrations
5. Easy to follow arguments
6. Right tone
7. Unusual stories and words
8. Personal writing — using the word "you"

Proofreading and editing tips: Refer to the writing guidelines and the QC guidelines in the process document.

Tips to handle writer's block: You are all set to start writing when all of a sudden your mind is a blank! A familiar feeling among all writers; a forlorn sensation of desolation and dread! Your article needs to be submitted in a few hours and your mind is stuck in a state of nothingness!

Well, it does not signal the end of your writing career nor does it mean the death of your article. Writer's block need not become the bane of your existence. All it requires is some mature handling. Read a book, go out and look at the garden, indulge in a hobby, play a game, chat with a friend, listen to music or do anything that can relax your mind, be it bungee jumping or curling up in bed and reading your favorite book! And if you are not willing to let go of your writing, then write by all means.

But, write about something else — about the ten favorite things you like (or hate!) about your spouse or your friends or your boss, the wonderful things you plan to buy with a million dollars or the first time you cooked a meal. You will soon find your creative juices flowing, and that article or essay will be easier to write.

Vocabulary Aids: When you come across a difficult word, look it up in the dictionary (place one on your desk or bookmark any online dictionary). Create your own list of words and store them in an accessible place. Use the new words that you learn in sentences while conversing with peers (as long as the words are used within context and people don't think that you are trying to show off your newfound knowledge, it's okay).

Promotional Copy: Because we are discussing selling ideas to people, we also need to look at promotional copywriting and what it takes to bring the marketing focus into a business article. What is promo-copy? It is writing that sells! It is writing that sells your services, a product or your brand. It also means getting listed on the search engines and ranking high on their lists.

Write down the keywords that are related to a topic and sprinkle them liberally in the article. Usability studies have shown that if your article is 500 words long, each keyword can be used (2-3% of 500) about 10 to 15 times in the article. It helps to use more keywords in the first paragraph of an article (search engine strategy). Persuasive marketing is much more than using the correct keywords. It also means using the right tone in the article, offering something of use to the reader and selling ideas in a way that hits home.

Strategic Advantage of White Papers

The White Paper has its origins in the diplomatic service where they were public policy statements. In those days, there were typically three papers: white papers; Grey papers were for informative purposes; and Black papers detailed disavowed clandestine activities. At the time, Government and Scientific bodies wrote white papers to enlighten their peers on a particular subject, for example, investigations into a new technology. These documents were supported with impartial, unbiased facts to aid in the decision-making process. The authors had no 'agenda' other than to assist their readers to understand the subject in question.

Such White Papers are now reserved for University research programs and Government think-thanks. In today's competitive landscape, the humble white paper has evolved into a different creature. In the IT industry, it is used to:

— Generate interest in new products

— Differentiate products and services from competitors offerings

— Demonstrate market leadership

— Promote authors are subject-matter experts

— Create news-flow for journalists

— Win business

White Papers are frequently based on market research, polls, or surveys that a company has carried out, or has sponsored in conjunction with a research firm. White Papers help convert prospective customers into paying customers.

Strategic Marketing Tools

In the IT world, these documents are critical to your company's survival, growth, and success. White Papers influence prospective customers. Not every customer will phone or email you about your products - but they will download your white papers-and case studies-and then read them at their convenience. According to market research, white papers are the first port-of-call for decision-makers when investigating a product.

Decision-makers, such as CIO's and IT Managers, are under tremendous pressure to make the correct choice when choosing a products and/or service. You can help them make that decision by producing persuasive arguments in your paper that demonstrates why your product/service fits their requirements. Your document helps them build a case for recommending your product to their superiors e.g. Board of Directors. It is for this reason, that graphs, charts and diagrams are so valuable. They will frequently be cut-and-pasted out of your documents and into the PowerPoint presentation that the CIO will make to his team.

Role of White Papers

Don't underestimate the role that white papers now have in the IT industry. For example, consider these facts:

1. White papers are the first external source of information consulted by decision-makers on a particular product.

2. White Papers are widely distributed amongst those in the decision-making process.

3. Executives often consult White Papers even before their own Sales team.

4. White papers provide critical input into the final decision about selected a product or service.

5. White papers have a very long shelf life. Magazines, newspapers and other material get discarded quite quickly; White papers, in contrast, get filed for future reference and remain for long periods on corporate intranets.

Use White Papers as strategic tools in your marketing arsenal and influence those in the decision-making process.

It's not easy to write a white paper. And reading them can also be quite a challenge! Unfortunately, many white papers are difficult to digest and come across as though slightly 'nerdy-types', locked in research labs, prepared them with very little consideration for their readers. So, if you're about to write your first white paper, here are a few golden rules to follow...

Get the Best Writer on board: Individuals with little writing experience are often delegated to write the white paper. In the IT industry, there is an assumption that the developer is best suited to write about the solution. Let's be honest: writers write and programmers program. There are some individuals who have both skills, but these are hard to find. In general, developers are not ideal for writing white papers; and neither is the Sales Manager.

Developers will focus on the technical innards, while sales types will gust about its 'unique' qualities. In doing so, both miss the mark. You can save yourself a lot of stress by hiring an experienced writer who can look at your product or service - and present it in an easy-to-understand manner. These writers know how to 'sell' a concept to both a technical and business audience-not everyone has this skill.

Sharp Presentation: Attractive graphics reinforce your message. Use diagrams and charts to stop 'glazed eyes syndrome' setting in. Text-heavy documents drain the reader very quickly! By combining charts, diagrams and tables you weave together the main selling points and sustain the reader's interest.

Avoid Terminology: Geekspeak and Three Letter Acronyms-e.g. B2B, B2G-are endemic in the IT industry. Experienced writers avoid TLAs as they know that readers won't understand the terminology, become frustrated and move on. If you have to use these terms, put a reference section at the start. No-one likes to be patronized. Technical terms without a clear definition will lose the reader's confidence in both you and your products. They will stop reading and go somewhere else. Why not? After all, your beloved White Paper is not the only show in town!

Subject Matter Organization: Before you get to the heart of the paper, outline the relevant background materials, such as industry research figures, that support your arguments. In the opening section, highlight why your solution exists; in other words, what specific problem does it solve? Don't meander from topic to topic or you will lose the reader. Each paragraph should only discuss one idea. Don't mix ideas in the same sentence or paragraph. For example, before you begin, assume that the reader is completely new to the subject matter. Then outline the most significant issues and progressively walk through the solution; begin with the larger issues first and sequentially move though the other points.

Abstract v. Reality: Many white papers discuss the theoretical application on the solution, e.g. Product X will do Y in situation Z. That's fine up to a point as it helps paint a picture for the reader. However, you need to underline your 'theory' with real world examples. Case studies and customers quotes are a very effective way of demonstrating how your solution performs in a working environment. Case studies reinforce the theoretical concepts. They help the reader see how the solution could work for them. If the reader can't relate to your solution in a practical sense, they will search elsewhere for another product.

Summary

Oddly enough, many of us read the summary first. Because of this, it should capture the essence of the white paper and identify the most interesting points. White Papers are a low-cost way to promote your products and potentially gain an advantage over your competitors. They also have a long shelf-life. They live on the web, intranets, and hard-drives long after your product has been rebranded, you've changed business strategy, or moved onto the golf course.

For this reason, ensure that your publication reflects positively on your company's high standards. Poor quality material will have the opposite effect of what you intended. Persistence is the key. Once you get it right, a well-written white paper pays for itself many times over in the long-term.

Grow Your Business by Writing Articles and White Papers

Recently we describe White Papers and their effectiveness in generating business opportunities. You might be interested in the following statistics, as they illustrate the returns you can generate from a well-crafted white paper. White paper marketing creates opportunities very fast. If you know your product, and your customers, then they will want to read your white paper, particularly when you write about a niche industry or service. To do this, a few points should be highlighted:

— White papers require an investment in research and writing time.

— White papers work well if you have a unique product with information your clients don't have.

— Writing white papers is not for everyone.

Be careful about who you chose to write the paper. Ultimately, white papers are strategic sales documents. Engineers can't write these. Don't ask them - it's not fair for you or them. They can contribute to the technical details, but you need to have an experienced writer managing the overall delivery and coordinating all resources involved. If, you do have experience in writing, it shouldn't take a lot of your time.

Most relatively experienced writers could write at least five good articles, (for example around 1000 words), with material that we have at hand.

Start with One Article

Choose the subject matter that is the easiest to write about, and will generate the most interest from your customer base. When writing sales-orientated articles, use a light conversational style as if you were talking to a friend. Though the article promotes your product or services, the sales angle is hidden in the helpful, useful information that you are providing to your readers i.e. your prospective client. Useful white papers build credibility and have a long shelf life. Decision-makers store them for as a reference.

Always, include a section at the end about yourself with your contact information, including 1800 telephone numbers and email address. Once you've written the article, get a reliable person to check the grammar and spelling. Make sure it's clear, concise, and to the point. Then, leave it aside for a day or two. This is a very useful trick. When you return to it later in the week, you'll have some distance and be able to see where it needs adjusting. Now, you're ready to use it for promotion-and that's what we'll talk about next month.

Designing White Papers

In the IT industry, the white paper has become a popular tool for promoting a product or service. It is frequently used in tandem with case studies, and other sales collateral, to promote a company's respective product of services. As with all writing, you first have to define your target audience. Once you have this organized, you can them begin to tailor your arguments towards their needs. It is important to stress this point, as many novice writers-especially those with a technical background-will focus on the low-level aspects of the software. Though this has its place, it's probably not here. Executives, and those in the management layer, are typical white papers readers. So, write with these readers in mind. You also need to determine the topic of your white paper. This may sound obvious but many writers overlook this and ramble from one vaguely related subject to the next.

Your white paper is intended to achieve several objectives:

— It needs to establish you as the definitive authority on the subject in question, i.e. that you stand head-and-shoulders above the competition in this area.

— It needs to create awareness of a new market trend and/ or a product offering that very specifically addresses a requirement. And it demonstrates how you are uniquely qualified to achieve this objective.

— It ensures that decision-makers select you over your competitors by providing them with persuasive arguments backed up with trustworthy references.

Structure of a White Paper

There are several sections required in every white paper:

— *Introduction*: this opening section covers the high-level issues and trends in the industry (or market sector) that you are involved with. It may also include the recommendations or conclusions that you have made about this main subject matter.

— *High Level Solution*: this describes the relevant technologies at a high level, especially tnose you have designed and intend to promote. In this section, it is recommended that you support your arguments with tables, charts, and graphics. All of these add weight to your argument and provide a contrast to the main text.

— *Solution Details*: this explains how the service, technology, or business model works. This is the heart of the white paper. You can also use tables, charts, and graphics for this section, with cross-references to external supporting documents if required.

— *Business benefits*: This includes areas such as ROI (return on investments), usability, adherence to international standards, and value-for money. Quotes for customers who have used your solution are always very helpful. It demonstrates that you have authority in this field and can back it up with an authentic reference. Don't take this for granted-not all your competitors will be able to supply such endorsements.

— *Summary*: close the paper with a concise summary of your main points. As many readers will skip the entire document and just read this section, you need to summarize here the main selling points about your solution. Write the summary as if it were an entirely standalone document. Distill the entire solution into this one page and conclude it with the single most important point that you want the reader to consider. If this section is compelling enough, you might persuade them to go back and read the entire document.

Finally, remember that your white paper is a primarily a sales document; it is not a technical manual. Once you have finished it, leave it aside for a few days. Then go back and read it. Ask yourself: would I buy this solution? Hopefully the answer is Yes. If not, don't be too hard on yourself as it takes time to write a persuasive white paper. Instead, identify the areas you feel are weak and go about strengthening them. Soon, you'll have a nice, sharp document that you can proudly stand over.

More Guidelines for Writing White Papers

1. *Put the conclusion at the start*: The introduction is the best place to summarize your findings - including the conclusions that you have made. Other publications, such as newspapers, use headlines and paragraph summaries to hold the reader's interest: white papers benefit from the same approach. Putting the conclusion at the end of your white paper make senses, but you need to be careful as this section is often overlooked by the reader, many of whom won't read to the very end.
2. *Customers are Investors*: Try to think of your customers are prospective investors. In addition, investors are a very discriminating audience. They judges technologies, products, and ideas based on objective information and the track record of those involved. They are hungry for real facts and will dismiss unsubstantiated claims. Maintaining their attention involves building trust and offering facts that are interesting, relevant, and true. They will look for trustworthy evidence to substantiate your claims. By providing this evidence, you not only save them time but also increase your credibility. Finding meaningful testimonials is well worth the effort.
3. *Avoid Assumptions*: Product descriptions written by product managers, web designers, or marketing directors often contain assumptions (and IT acronyms) that are understood only by their peers. You need to avoid this at all costs. Your readers will not understand these cryptic references and feel excluded. Before getting into the details of your solution, describe the high-level requirements first. Start with the essentials:

— Is it hardware or software?

— What are the prerequisites?

— What platform is it designed for?

— Where language is it written in?

— Who will use the solution

4. *Be Specific*: After providing this preliminary information, get to the main issues. If you know that your readers are, for example, technology experts then don't try to teach them about the basics. They'll just skip past these sections. Generalities and bland repetition drives such readers away. Instead, describe specific aspects that will ring true with your audience.

5. *Differentiate*: It's one thing to claim your product solves a problem, but it's more convincing to describe how it does this. You need to provide evidence that your solution is better than your rivals are-and then substantiate this with, for example, benchmark tests.

6. *Balance Text v. Graphics*: Use graphics, tables, and charts to help the reader understand your product. Graphics are ideal for illustrating the relationship between concepts, technologies, and systems. Also, remember that the readers will tire after several pages; graphics, tables and charts serve as an alternative to the text while still maintaining their interest in the subject.

7. *Use Clear English*: Though the IT industry is global, many readers learned English as a second language. Such readers tend to get confused by lengthy sections, complex sentences, and new buzzwords. Instead, try to use simple, plain English. Such writing carries real power-the power to explain and convince. If the best ingredient for an effective white paper is a terrific solution to a technical problem, then the next best ingredient is great writing.

Difference between Features and Benefits

When you are writing about a product or service, you need to understand the difference between features and benefits. You have to get this right, as the customer's response is based on:

1. How you converted feature into benefits and
2. How you sold those benefits to them.

The main features of Microsoft Word, for example, are its word processing capabilities, such as the ability to Save as HTML, use Templates and spell-check the document. Even though customers want to know the main features, they BUY the benefits. Features relate to the seller, and benefits relate to the buyer. Prospective customers ask themselves: how do I benefit from this product or service? and will it increase my sales, reduce manual operations, or improve my business?

First off, look at the product/service from their perspective. When discussing benefits, use the "you" language technique. For example, let's improve this feature-centric statements with "you" language:

1. Our new product has 1000 time-reducing features
2. Product Z is user-friendly.
3. Our website has the fastest download times.

If you write this from the buyer's perspective, it reads:

1. You'll earn $1000 a month.
2. You'll learn this accounting software in 5 minutes.

From now on, when you are writing sales material, try to convert dry features into sticky consumer benefits. Your sales team will notice the results.

Ten Tips on Writing White Papers

Technical writers are often asked to contribute to their

company's white papers. Sometimes a product manager will write the paper and a technical writer will edit it; other times the writer will generate the text. These completed papers are usually posted on the company's Web site and distributed to potential customers at trade shows and meetings. Following are ten suggestions for improving results.

1. *Analyze Your Audience*: Before you begin writing, define your audience. You might even want to include a section called "Intended Audience" in the body of the paper. An audience analysis will reveal the extent to which you must explain technical concepts. The results of this analysis will determine not only the level of technical content but also your writing style. For example, if your white paper is pitching a brand new technology to business development experts (as opposed to engineers), you should take care to explain the technology in language your audience can understand.

2. *Create an Outline*: Your outline will vary depending on your subject, but generally it's a good idea to structure your white paper so that it presents a solution to a problem. You could use an introductory section to define the problem, and then describe your solution in the body of the document. Ideally, you should have a subject matter expert, a marketing representative, and a member of your potential audience review the outline. This spares you the pain of removing sections because "that window didn't make it into the release" or "we're not pitching that feature right now."

3. *Use Diagrams Carefully*: While a picture may be worth a thousand words, a diagram often requires a thousand-word explanation. Clear, professional-looking diagrams are invaluable, but overly complex diagrams tend to look silly and can often confuse readers. There's nothing worse than the "hockey puck object models" and "Dadaist program architectures" that we find in industry

documents. You should also make sure that all diagrams in a document are of similar quality. The authority of a white paper is diminished when a colorful, professional "marketecture" diagram is followed by a technical diagram whipped up by one of the developers in Microsoft Word.

4. *Explore a Less Formal Writing Style*: Unfortunately, most white papers are less compelling than most user manuals-and that's not a compliment to user manuals. Because white papers are marketing documents, they should be not merely readable but riveting. Don't be afraid to use metaphors, contractions, humor, and other devices. This doesn't necessarily mean writing in dialect or using other verbal fireworks to get attention: It simply means minimizing the technical lingo and inserting the occasional analogy. One of the best white papers I've read used a can of black beans to explain the basics of XML.

5. *Solve a Problem*: Too many white papers are extended brochures that offer minute detail about features but don't explain why the reader might want the product. Your white paper should tell a simple but compelling story about how your company, product, or feature particularly and uniquely unravels the reader's Gordian knot. For example, instead of writing "Buy a DVD player because it has 128-bit oversampling and advanced virtual surround sound," you'd be better off with "Buy a DVD player because you need better sound and a crisper picture."

6. *Beware of Marketing-Speak*: As technical writers, we're the first readers who can sniff out the vague adjectives that sometimes accumulate in white papers. If potential customers have gone to the trouble of actually procuring your document, they want to know what your product does and why they should buy it.

7. *Supply Supporting Evidence*: Quotations from your customers are valid, but everyone knows they are often

solicited and tweaked to fit a company's message. It's more valuable to provide third-party information that supports your proposed solution. For example, if your company's DVD player has an embedded clock, you might state that a reputable survey reports that "80 percent of VCR owners cannot set their VCR clock."

8. *Introduce and Summarize*: An effective, compelling introduction is crucial, and should obviate need for an "executive summary"-the synopsis that precedes the table of contents in most white papers. These summaries have little value: Your audience may not consist solely of suit-wearing bigwigs with too little time to read the whole document, and the non-executives in your audience may resent the implication that these summaries are not for them. At the end of the document, be sure to repeat the problem and summarize how your product addresses it. Too many white papers peter out after the last feature.
9. *Spiff It Up (Appearance Is Important)*: In terms of style and length, a white paper has a lot in common with a magazine article, so it should receive similar graphic treatment. Use all of the usual designer's tools-text boxes, columns, pull quotes, graphics, and so forth-to create an attractive, readable document.
10. *Trim It Down (It's Probably Too Long)*: Even if you've followed all this advice, your white paper isn't going to get more attention than a Stephen King novel, or even the reader's e-mail. The shorter your paper, the better. The length of the paper depends on the complexity of your product and method. If you can't say what is necessary in that space, perhaps you need to divide your message into more than one document.

Most people drastically underestimate the time and effort it takes to produce a decent, readable white paper. While this list is not exhaustive, it may help you avoid a few common pitfalls.

6

Easy-to-read Writing

Technical writing requires clarity of expression and therefore simplicity of language. Technical writing is intent on expressing certain key concepts so that these may be understood as easily as possibly by the intended readers - be they programmers or users. Writing in a clear, concise manner makes not only understanding the text easier for the reader, it also makes your life as a writer of technical documentation easier - especially when you are not a native speaker of English. When talking about algorithms, or sequences of events in a program, absolute clarity of writing is not only needed in the code discussed.

The understanding of written text depends on three distinct components:

— Legibility

— Readability

— Comprehensibility

The first of these components is of no concern to us, as it is a responsibility of the layouters and typesetters putting our writing into its final form. The second of these we will deal with, as it is vital to having the reader actually read our document, hopefully in full. And lastly, the third component is essential to ensure that our reader will understand the purpose of our writing. These two components will be discussed in separate sections, even though some of the issues raised may be pertinent to both. In addition, we will also look at issues of style - some of writing's do's and don'ts, as even the prose of technical writing does not have to be equivalent to a blunt axe when it might be an instrument of precision.

Readability

The concepts of readability and comprehensibility imply that the act of reading beyond the physical act of seeing and deciphering characters and chunks of text is vastly more complex. As the next step beyond this 'raw' level of input, we need to assume a process of tokenising, akin to what a compiler does with the source code of a given program. This process of tokenising is what readability is concerned with. Thus, our writing will need to meet a number of requirements to successfully pass this stage:

1. The sentences must be well formed syntactically
2. The sentences must not exceed a certain length
3. The sentences should not be below a minimum length
4. Recursion must be kept to a minimum
5. The choice of words should vary

If a technical text is unreadable in the reader's eye, he will quite probably assume that the product described in this text also is of inferior quality. Code is a language, just as the language of the documentation is. Not writing well in documentation implies faults in coding style. Therefore, readability is an absolute requirement for documentation of successful products.

Well formed Sentences

By well formed sentences, we do not merely mean that the sentences should conform to grammatical rules of the

English language, but also that they are clearly built. We will now look at some negatives and discuss solutions:

This sentence no verb: Glaring grammatical errors such as omitting a vital component of the sentence - in this case the verb - should be avoided at all cost. Read out loud, whenever in doubt. Usually, these mistakes occur in longer, more convoluted sentences. Check these twice when they cannot be rewritten in split-up form.

This sentence does a verb have: Never, ever try to transpose a grammatical construct of your mother tongue into a literal English equivalent - even more so in cases of colloquialisms, as above! If you are able to translate a sentence word by word back into your mother tongue, you most probably made a severe mistake or two in writing it. Read texts by native speakers of English. Rewrite your own text next, and then reread it.

In this case, we see that there is, as such, a larger than necessary number of commas: Punctuation should be kept to a minimum. It is not necessary to put a comma wherever it looks right. They often are not. Especially clauses of the 'so that' type can do perfectly well without commas. This rule of course also holds for all other punctuation. And never, ever, try to transport punctuation rules from your native tongue to the English you are writing.

Of course, many more cases of sentences not well formed might be constructed, but quite probably you will find enough of these when looking through various pieces of writing. And not only will you find these in non-native writers of English. Therefore, again - read what others wrote!

Overlong Sentences

Often we encounter sentences which run on too long. Understanding such sentences is extremely difficult, as short term memory has a very limited capacity. Similar to the rule that telephone numbers may not have more than 5 digits plus/minus two, sentences should not exceed a certain length. It is given as a rule, which however is not the only such rule you may encounter, that sentences should not exceed a desirable length of ten to fifteen words, never should fall below seven words or extend beyond the ultimate limit of tolerable length reached at twenty words, even though longer sentences may be found in high literature, where even punctuation as it is used in this example to facilitate reading is oft omitted in novel experimental ways.

This of course is an example that runs somewhat longer than what you would expect to find in your own writing. But read your own texts again and you will quite possibly find one or two of these abominations, describing say, a complex chain of events and their handling. A complex train of thought can only benefit from being broken down into sentences of convenient length. Temptation to ramble on in one long sentence may be great. Resist. Your logic will benefit. Also cut out anything not necessary to the immediate cause at hand.

Short Sentences

Short sentences are easily read, but tend to look breathless and overly excited. Sentences may be short. Then they are easy to read. And understand, too. But they look cheap. And breathless. As well as leaving the reader restless. Not much needs to be said here, as these above sentences illustrate the point to be made. If a thing is worth saying, it is worth saying it well, not chopping language to pieces. Human language is not a RISC language. Interesting writing depends on well dosed variations of length and choice of words - for examples of the latter.

Recursion

Sentences often turn into a quasi-circular case of recursion while reading them when the references made in the sentence to the respective objects and subjects are left unclear by using the same pronoun to describe these subjects and objects.

It is not easy to understand it when it is unclear what is referenced by 'it' - it by now should be clear what it is supposed to mean, isn't it?

In such a case, replace one - preferably the first - instance of each subject/object referenced by 'it' with its actual name. This will make reading much easier. Recursion of this type often also is an indication of laziness on the writer's part, as it hints at an unwillingness to formulate a thought properly. This however is only a short term saving of effort, as readers probably will contact the author asking for clarification and thus causing more unproductive work on the writer's part than necessary. Another form of recursion will take place in the reader's mind when he is confronted with convoluted sentences containing insertions, ellipses and other rhetoric figures. All of these will need some place on his 'stack' - and a reader's stack is shallow. 'Pushing' and 'popping' more than three stack levels usually ends in disaster ... for the message of your sentence!

The reader, that is, the intended recipient of our text, a hopefully clearly written and logically structured document, will, if he is able to fully understand our prose, without difficulty come to a safe assumption of what any given sentence, such as this a one, conveys, to him, the reader, by the way of meaning. The above sentence is grammatically correct, but will most probably provoke a 'stack overflow' in our average reader. Such convolutedwriting should be avoided wherever possible. Just as recursive code, text may be 'flattened out'. Take a monster such as the one above apart. Shorter sentences make easier reading. If this is not possible, try to keep related parts of the sentences as close to each other as possible.

Choice of Words

Reading is a process that takes its toll on the reader. This task should therefore be made as easy as possible for him. Making reading an easier task, if not a pleasure, can be achieved by varying the vocabulary used to describe the topics at hand. Using the same words all over to describe the same things again and again is not pleasant even more so when we can use different words to replace those same words we are using again and again to describe the same thing in the same words. For any given word, at least one synonym will be available. Do not hesitate to use a thesaurus. Also, do not use the exact same phrasing again and again and again, unless it is intended to convey some artistic intention - this however is almost never the case in technical writing.

Comprehensibility

In the complex process of reading, the step following the 'tokenisation' of the text is the actual 'parsing' - understanding what these symbols and their relations mean. A clear separation of these two steps however can not be made.

— A great portion of comprehensibility issues already was covered when we discussed recursion

— Recursion is the enemy of understanding

An understandable technical document always follows a logical structure. Any topic discussed is based on the preceding topics. If a new concept is needed for the topic at hand, it needs to be introduced before using it in dealing with this new topic. This holds true for any level of detail of the document at hand, down to individual sentences. The basic steps are:

1. Definition
2. Assumption/Theorem

3. Explanation/Proof
4. Conclusion

Of course, the classic structure of 'thesis, antithesis, synthesis' may be more appropriate for certain topics, such as discussion of architectural decisions, but generally the above sequence is exactly what we need. On the 'atomic' level of a sentence, its logical structure is governed by raw grammar. Therefore, a good working knowledge of grammar is absolutely necessary for getting our ideas across to the reader as we mean them to be.

Definition

In this segment of the document, all terms and concepts necessary for the following should be defined. In some cases, reference to previous material in the document is sufficient. If it should for some reason be necessary, the definitions may be placed in endnotes or a glossary at the end of the document. This should be clearly indicated at the very beginning of the document. Footnotes are not intended for the purpose of definitions. They are a place for further explanations or material of a 'non sequitur' nature.

Assumption/Theorem

The task of this segment is the presentation of the idea or concept this particular document or part of a document is supposed to deal with. Make a simple and clear cut statement of where your argument starts and what will be the intended outcome.

Explanation/Proof

It may be of purely argumentativenature - say, defending architectural decisions - or come close to mathematical proof in style. In the case of a program implemented practically, this is the place for explaining the workings of it step by step. Or in the case of a user's guide, to explain the interface and sequence of steps necessary for completing a given task.

Conclusion

For the document to be successful, a conclusion must be given, reiterating the above steps in a shortened form. This will reinforce the impact of the material presented on the reader. The human mind, unlike a computer, needs to be told several times before committing to a certain course of action. Repeat the central message of what you write several times. The human mind is not at ease when confronted with a 'fire and forget' type of message.

Matters of Style

This section will be concerned with the little things that will hopefully turn acceptable technical writing into good writing. There is a number of seemingly small and unobtrusive 'do's' and 'don'ts' that need to be watched out for consciously even though they seem to be obvious. The following material is not sorted by relevance. You will just find things as they came to mind, read through it and consider it as a wish list for good writing.

Title

The first thing our reader sees is the title. Therefore, the appearance of the title is of great importance for the impression our text leaves. The dominating factor is capitalisation of the words in the title. There are several 'schools of tought' as far as this is concerned:

1. All Words In Titles Are Capitalised
2. Only the first word is capitalised
3. nothing is capitalised
4. First Word and all Nouns are capitalised

Big Words

Don't go above your station. It may well be tempting to employ vocabulary gleaned from some obscure manual of language, obfuscating your intent by billowing clouds of rhetoric smoke, this however will most certainly induct the reader's total non-comprehension of your text. By now it should be clear what the name of the game is: in the case of two given words of the same meaning, preferably use the simpler one. With one exception: should the 'bigger' word be clearer as to its meaning, use that.

And when you find yourself in the 'Big Word Game', also check the length of your sentences. There seems to be a correlation between the two. However, you will find that using only the smallest possible word to refer to a concept will making your writing look dull. A bit of variety never hurts.

It's...

It's often a matter of confusion for non-native speakers to decide when to use 'its' and when to use 'it's'. The former is the genitive of 'it', the latter is a contraction of 'it is'. Simple. When in doubt, check back here. And preferably write 'it is', as this makes for better style than 'it's', without too much extra typing effort. This way, the problem of what form to use will vanish automagically, anyway.

An 'a'

It is of course somewhat tempting when trying to write good English to use 'a' and 'an' in accordance with the simple assumption that 'a' is to be used before consonants and 'an' before vowels. This is not in accordance with the rules of proper English. Simple (assumed) rules usually have exceptions to prove them in general. The exception in this case is with vowels:

— An apple

— An exception

— An idea

— A useless rule but

— An uppercase letter

This is of course a mere rule of thumb. For the full story refer to a style manual such as 'The King's English'.

Do not Use 'Don't'

The use of contracted negated verbs is something that should not be done in good technical writing. Writing out a negation in full does not take much effort on the writer's part and leaves the impression of a writer caring about his style. Should he also be the coder of the program documented, attention to such details will also affect the perception of the quality of his coding style by the reader. So: no won't, can't, don't, isn't, aren't, couldn't, shouldn't; And never, ever: ain't, shan't

Can, Could, etc.

Coming from a German language background will lead to a very specific problemwith the various meanings of the versatile German auxiliary verb 'können' when translating it into English.

— *Can*: the ability to perform an action - after having initialised foo, we now can call bar(baz)

— Could: a possibility, or rarely in the case of technical writing, the past tense of can in the case of an exception being thrown, we could catch it, or dismiss it.

— *May*: a speculative possibility - in future versions of foo, we may implement bar().

— *Might*: an alternative - instead of calling foo(), we might call bar() when the following conditions ... are fulfilled.

Nativisms

In general, be suspicious of 'too obviously natural' translations of words from your native tongue into English. E.g., the German 'Konkurrenz' will translate to English as 'competition', not as 'concurrence' as might be naively assumed. Get a good dictionary and check it often, read English texts you are already familiar with in your tongue - no matter whether that text is originally English translated to your native tongue or vice versa. Preferably start with some favourite book of yours - be that 'The Lord of the Rings', 'Grimm's Fairy Tales' or 'Gödel, Escher, Bach' or even comic strips or whatever else has taken your fancy. Understanding words properly matters. When in doubt about the actual use of a word with several potential meanings in translation, check with a native speaker or refer to a good reference dictionary such as the 'Oxford'.

Ego Trip

Never, ever, use the word 'I' in technical writing. It is anathema. We are dealing with objective matters, not personal opinions. 'I' may only be used when voicing very personal opinions which usually do not belong into a document of technical importance - when discussing design decisions made by you, 'I' may be used legitimately, but not when describing a technical detail such an in interface. When engaged in a flame war, 'I' is perfectly fine, but not anywhere else near a technical topic. Should you however feel a burning urge to use 'I', switch over to the passive voice or third person writing.

Turning to impersonal writing worked well for Caesar, when he was giving his account of his personal accomplishments in the Gallic wars - this account is considered classic literature, even though it in fact is very technical writing. The passive voice is to be avoided in general, as it makes for tiring reading, but in such cases as we are now discussing, it is preferable to endless 'I think..., I consider this to ..., I did...'. Whenever possible, use 'we' to forge a bond between you and the reader. This will give a feeling of 'being in it together'. Classical technical writing is very much bound and impersonal style in general. This nowadays is no longer true. But still, technical writing is not a 'family thing'!

When to Use 'If'

Conditional clauses may be begun with 'when' or 'if'. Confusion sometimes comes from the problem of when to use which. With a bit of thinking, the distinction between these two cases is simple:

— *When*: used in cases of a temporal conditional - when the sun rises, the cock crows

— If: used in the case of a causal conditional - if we manage to get out of this text alive...

This Sentence Does Overdo it

Using 'do' as an auxiliary verb usually does more harm than help. It tends to overemphasise sentences - especially with 'weak' verbs such as 'have' it gives the impression of speaking just that little bit too loud. Using 'do' as in the introductory sentence of this paragraph as a verb by itself is in order. But it does give a certain obnoxious quality of overassertiveness to your writing if you do use it as an auxiliary verb when you definitely do not need to use it to say what you do want to say. Now that does settle this point, does it not?

Time is on our Side

Always try to keep the (grammatical) tense of technical

documents in the present. Past tense ought to be out of the question, as we generally are not concerned with past developments.

Consistency

Be consistent in the use of either British or US-english spelling. Never switch inside any given document. Examples of difference in spelling between those two are:

British	US
Colour	Color
Co-operation	Cooperation
Customisation	Customization

Also, once you choose a given technical term to mean one thing, use it only in that one sense. Do not redefine!

Editor's Pet Peeves

At some point in any writer's life comes the moment where his work is submitted to an editor. This breed of person does have a lot of experience with language and the common weaknesses of the technical writer. Over time it has become clear that the same mistakes are made again and again. So, save them time and yourself humiliation by following the list below. It contains additional material not covered above. To make things easier, the list is organized by topic.

The most important issues or the most commonly misused terms are bolded. The words in this list are supposed to be spelled as printed here, including capitalisation, hyphenation or lack thereof, and separated or not as given. Also note that US-english is the reference here, as opposed to the other text, as almost all technical writing is published by American publishing houses.

Grammar and logic

—*allow vs enable*: People allow; objects enable. Some editors are more stringent about this rule than others. - Georgie allowed me to borrow his CD. The program enabled me to create a stunning document. You might also consider to use let as synonym for allow. - He let me borrow his CD.

— *although vs while vs whereas*: Use while only when describing the action of doing two things simultaneously. Use although and whereas for contrast.

— *Figures*: The first reference to a figure should always be before it is presented.

— Ensure that the spellingof terminology in figures is same as in the text. Captions (please remember to include them) should be informative sentences. - bad caption: The File Open dialog box. good caption: In the File Open dialog box we... When referenced in the text with a specific number, the term 'Figure' is always capitalized.

— *graphic (n)*: The noun form usually takes a singular verb.

— *graphics (adj)*: Use graphics as an adjective in relation to the field of graphic art or graphic design - graphics file is ok.

— *once vs after vs when*: Use once for time references. Use after to show that an event has already taken place. Use when to show actions or events that are occurring simultaneously.

— *over vs more than*: Over denotes crossing a barrier or exceeding a limit. More than qualifies a number. - She has worked more than 60 hours this week.

— *preceding vs previous*: Preceding means immediately before in time and place. Previous means simply earlier, prior, or before, but not necessarily immediately before. For example, if the current month is June, the preceding month is May; previous months are January through April.

— *since vs because*: Use since for time references. Use because when explaining the reasons why something happened.

— *There is, There are/ Here is, Here are*: Sentences starting with this construction are usually more clear and less wordy if they're rewritten.

Spelling and terminology

— above, below: Avoid this terminology when referring to figures or other references. Instead, be specific or use preceding, following, next and so on.

— backward, toward, forward (no "s" on any of these words)

— check box, check mark

— back up (v); backup (n)

— clip art

— Clipboard

— CompuServe

— Control Panel

— Ctrl key (spelled as it is on the keyboard)

— Ctrl+Alt+Delete vs Ctrl-Alt-Delete: On the PC, keystroke sequences are separated by plus signs. In Mac texts, sequences are separated by hyphens. This however, is subject to variation depending on the editor's preferences.

— desktop

— disc vs disk: Use disc when referring to a CD or an optical; Use disk when referring to a 3 ½- or 5 ¼-inch disk. Never use diskette.

— double-click, right-click, left-click (always hyphenated as verb)

— drop-down (adj, n); drop down (v)

— email: no hyphen, no capitalization

— filename

— home page

— hotkey (one word): Make sure that hotkeys are marked in the chapters. Hotkeys are indicated typographically.

— HTML: Hypertext Markup Language (notice that the "t" in Hypertext is lowercase)

— inline

— intranet is lowercase; Internet is uppercase

— ISP: Internet service provider (no need to make the "s" and the "p" uppercase)

— keyword

— log in/login vs log on/logon: Both forms are acceptable, but be consistent. As a verb, log in or log on are two words. As an adjective, login and logon are one word.

— Measurements

bps	bit per second
GHz	gigahertz
Hz	hertz
KB	kilobyte
Kb	kilobit
Kbps	kilobits per second
KHz	kilohertz
MB	megabyte
Mb	megabit

Mbps	megabits per second
MHz	megahertz
ms	millisecond

— As for Kilobytes, be consistent in using either decimal (1K=1000) or power of two (1K=1024) notation. The former is to be preferred for physics, the later for computer science contexts. This also holds true for higher powers (mega, giga, tera, peta).

— menu bar

— multi, non, re, sub, and co prefixes: It's almost always safe to assume that you don't need to hyphenate these words. (For example, the correct spelling is multicolumn, not multi-column.) A few exceptions to note are as follows:

resort vs re-sort: Resort means a place of retreat; re-sort means to sort again.

recreate vs re-create: Recreate means to cut loose; to play.

Re-create means to create again.

resent vs re-sent: Resent means to show displeasure or indignation because of a feeling of being injured or offended. Re-sent means you sent something again.

There are a few exceptions in British usage though, such as co-operation. Settle the reference spelling context once and for all when you begin writing.

— Net - uppercase when referring to Internet,.NET or.net - all upper or lower case when referring to the Microsoft technologies, be consistent with the choice for the latter term.

— newsgroup

— offline, online

— offscreen, onscreen

— pathname

— Plug and Play

— PostScript

— pull-down menu

— ScanDisk

— scrollbar

— set up (v); setup (n, adj)

— Spacebar

— status bar

— Tables: Be specific when titling tables, and use sentence style capitalization (only first word and any proper nouns are capitalized) for table heads. As with figures, the word Table should be capitalized when a specific table is being mentioned, but lowercase when the reference is generic (The following table...). An ending period is no longer used after the table number in any series.

— taskbar

— terminology: Consistent use and capitalization of terminology is important. A novice reader as well as a general tech editor won't always have the knowledge or the software about which you write and thus won't always be able to catch technical inconsistencies.

— title bar

— ToolTip, ScreenTip

— TrueType font

— UNIX

— up-to-date (always hyphenated)

— URL: uniform resource locator ("u" stands for uniform, not universal).

— Usenet

— username

— Web - is always uppercase)

— wizard: Use uppercase "w" when talking about specific wizard and lowercase "w" when talking about generic

— worldwide (one word, unless referring to World Wide Web)

7

Common Page Design

Page design means different things to different people, but here it will mean the use typographical and formatting elements such as the following:

— Headings

— Lists

— Notices

— Tables

— Highlighting

— Margins, indentation & alignment

— Fonts & color

Headings

Headings are the titles and subtitles you see within the actual text of much professional scientific, technical, and business writing. Headings are like the parts of an outline that have been pasted into the actual pages of a report or other document. Headings are an important feature of professional technical writing: they alert readers to upcoming topics and subtopics, help readers find their way around in long reports and skip what they are not interested in, and break up long stretches of straight text.

Headings are also useful for writers. They keep you organized and focused on the topic. When you begin using headings, your impulse may be to slap in the headings after you've written the rough draft. Instead, visualize the headings before you start the rough draft, and plug them in as you write.

Guidelines for Headings

Here are some specific guidelines on headings

— Use headings to mark off the boundaries of the major sections and subsections of a report.

— Try for 2 to 3 headings per regular page of text. Don't overdo headings: for example, a heading for each of a series of one- or two-sentence paragraphs. (Also, you don't need a heading per every paragraph; normally, an individual heading applies to multiple paragraphs.)

— For short documents, begin with the second-level heading; skip the first-level.

— Make the phrasing of headings parallel. (See the section on parallelism for details.)

— Make the phrasing of headings self-explanatory: instead of "Background" or "Technical Information," make it more specific, such as "Physics of Fiber Optics."

— Make headings indicate the range of topic coverage in the section. For example, if the section covers the design and operation of a pressurized water reactor, the heading "Pressurized Water Reactor Design" would be incomplete and misleading.

— Avoid "lone" headings-any heading by itself within a section without another like it in that same section. For example, avoid having a second-level heading followed by only one third-level and then by another second-level. (The third-level heading would be the lone heading.)

— Avoid "stacked" headings-any two consecutive headings without intervening text.

— Avoid pronoun reference to headings. For example, if you have a third-level heading "Torque," don't begin the sentence following it with something like this: "This is a physics principle....."

— When possible, omit articles from the beginning of headings. For example, "The Pressurized Water Reactor" can easily be changed to "Pressurized Water Reactor" or, better yet, "Pressurized Water Reactors."

— Don't use headings as lead-ins to lists or as figure titles.

— Avoid "widowed" headings: that's where a heading occurs at the bottom of a page and the text it introduces start at the top of the next page. Keep at least two lines of body text with the heading, or force it to start the new page.

Designing Your Headings

If you want to use your own style and format of headings, contact your instructor. Together, you two may be able to work out alternate heading specifications. If you design your own style of headings, remember that the fundamental principle of heading design has to do with decreasing noticeability of headings, the lower the heading level.

In any heading style, you'll notice the top-level heading (first-level) is the largest, darkest, boldest, most highly visible heading on the page. The tools you can use to achieve this greater or lesser degree of visibility include bold, italics, type size, different fonts, relationship to surrounding text, graphics elements attached to headings, and so on. When you design your own heading style, be careful about going overboard with fancy typographical elements. Also, continue to use the guidelines; they apply to practically any design. And finally, use your heading design consistently throughout your document.

Lists

Lists are useful tools for emphasizing important points, enabling rapid scanning of text, and providing more white space. Some of the standard guidelines on lists are the followings:

— Use numbered lists for items that are in a required order or that must be referred to by number. Use bulleted lists for items in no required order.

— Use standard numbered- and bulleted-list format. Use standard HTML tagging for these types of lists so that numbers use the "1." style; bullets are the standard large dot; there is an adequate indent from the number or bullet to the text; and run-over lines indent properly.

— Make the phrasing of list items parallel.

— Introduce all lists with a lead-in; don't use headings as lead-ins to lists.

— Unless some internal style overrides, punctuate list items with a period only if they are complete sentences or have embedded dependent clauses.

— Use either initial cap or lowercase on the first word of list items, but do so consistently.

— For nested lists, use a bolded en dash for the bullet symbol in second-level list items; use lowercase letters for second-level numbered list items. Make sure that nested items align to the text or the previous level.

— Avoid excessive use of lists of lists with too many items. Seven to ten items is generally considered about the maximum for lists. On a standard page, there probably shouldn't be more than two or three lists, and at least three or four lines of regular text should come between them.

Notices

Notices are those specially formatted chunks of text that alert readers to potential problems or danger. The following presents some of the standard guidelines for notices.

— Use a standard hierarchy of notices in which notices are more prominent and noticeable as they become more severe.

— Consider using this hierarchy: danger notices for situations involving potential severe injury or fatality; cautions for situations involving minor injury; warnings for situations involving damage to equipment or data or threat to the success of the procedure; and notes for points of exception or emphasis not involving the preceding situations.

— Whatever notice design you use, avoid extended text in all bold, all italics, all-caps, or combinations thereof.

— In addition to telling readers to do or not to do something, explain what will happen if they ignore the warning, under what conditions to make use of the statement, how to recover if the statement is ignored.

— Make the text of notices succinct, but not at the expense of clear writing. Avoid telegraphic writing style in notices.

— In numbered lists, align notices to the text of the list item they apply to.

— The standard wisdom of placing notices before the step in which the potential problem exists can cause problems in formatting. If possible, state warnings, cautions or dangers at the beginning of the entire procedure.

Tables

Tables a like vertical lists, discussed previously, but more structured and formal. In your text, look for repeating pairs, triplets, or quadruplets of items that can be formatted as tables. For example, a series of terms and definitions is a classic use for tables. Some of the standard guidelines for tables.

— Look for repeating groups of items in your text that you can format as tables.

— Use a table title unless the content of the table is utterly obvious and the table contains few items. Make the table title the top row of the table.

— Use column and row headings (or both) to define the contents of the columns and rows. Consider using some sort of highlighting for these column and row headings.

— Left-align text columns (unless they are simple alphabetic character items). Left-align text columns with their headings.

— Right-align or decimal align numerical data, and center it under its heading.

— Put standard measurement units in the column or row heading rather than with each item in the column or row.

Highlighting

Software documentation typically uses a lot of highlighting. Highlighting here refers to bold, italics, alternate fonts, caps, quotation marks, and other such typographical tricks used to call attention to text. Some of the standard guidelines for highlighting are given below:

— Establish a plan for use of highlighting, and apply it consistently. Use highlighting for specific, functional reasons. Avoid too much highlighting; avoid complicated highlighting schemes.

— Consider using this fairly standard highlighting scheme:

  — For simple emphasis, use italics.

— Use bold for commands, on-screen buttons and menu options

— Use italics for variables for which users must supply their own words.

— Use an alternate font for text displayed on screen or text that users must type in.

— For screen and field names, use the capitalization style shown on the screen but no other highlighting.

— Use an initial cap for key names but no other highlighting.

— For extended emphasis, use the notice format.

Margins, Indentation and Alignment

A nice touch is to indent text one to two inches while leaving headings on the left margins. This style does two things: it makes the headings stand out, and it shortens the line length of regular text. In many instances, lines on web browser are fair too long to be comfortably readable. As a web page designer, you cannot ultimately control line length, but there are a few tricks you can try. You can use the "hanging-head" format in which all text is indented one to two inches while the headings remain on the left margin. You can also use the two-column variation in which headings are in a left column and text is in a right column.

Fonts and Color

On web pages, you can use color easily. You can also use whichever fonts your readers have available on their own computers. Obviously, you can't know which fonts readers have available to them, so you must choose the most common. Here are some suggestions concerning fonts and color:

— Use only the most common fonts—some readers may not have the same fonts that you do.

— Use only one alternate font, at most two. For example, you might use Arial for headings, Times New Roman for body text, and Courier New for text that displays on screen or that users must type in.

— Be careful with smaller type sizes and unusual fonts—make sure they are readable on other computer systems. In particular, check the appearance on a Mac if you are using a PC and vice versa; check the appearance on Microsoft Internet Explorer if you are using Netscape and vice versa.

— If you use color, use it minimally. For example, if you have black text on a white background, you might select another color for headings. You might use that same color for figure and table titles as well as the tags for notices.

— Again, as with fonts, check the alternate colors you've chosen on a variety of computer hardware to ensure its readability.

— Avoid unusual combinations of background and text colors. For example, purple or red text on a black background is horrible to read. Stick with black text on a white or gray background unless there is strong function reason for some other color combination.

8

Book Design

Book design means the content, style, format, design, and sequence of the various typical components of a book. "Components" here refers to actual sections or pages of a book such as the edition notice, the preface, the index, or the front or back cover. In the page-design chapter, the term element refers to things that can occur multiple times practically anywhere in a book, such as headers, footers, tables, illustrations, lists, notices, highlighting, and so on.

Certainly, no single user guide, technical reference manual, quick-reference document, or other such document would actually have all of these components designed and sequenced in precisely the way you are about to read. Book design components include:

- Front and back covers
- Title page
- Edition notice
- Disclaimers
- Trademarks
- Warranties
- Safety notices
- Communication statements

— Table of contents

— List of figures

— Preface

— Body chapters

— Appendixes

— Glossary

— Index

— Reader-response form

— Book design and layout

Front and back covers: Product documents for paying customers usually have nicely designed front covers even if, on the inside, the book is bargain basement in terms of its quality. On the front cover, you will typically see:

— Company name

— Product name

— Product platform or operating system

— Product version and release numbers

— Book title

— Company or product logos

— Trademark symbols

— Artwork

— Book order number

— Company or product slogan

It can be challenging to figure out a good format for the company name, product name, and book title. Sometimes, these can amount to a whole paragraph of text! Companies are quite divided on whether to indicate version and release numbers on front covers-some do; some don't. Almost always, however, you'll see the platform indicated-whether the product is for the Macintosh, the PC, UNIX, and so on.

The back cover of hardcopy user guides and manuals are usually very simple. typically, they contain the book order number, the name of the company with appropriate trademark symbols, a copyright symbol and phrasing as to the ownership of the book, and a statement as to which country the book was printed in. You'll also find bar codes on the back cover. See if your software can generate a bar code-you just access the bar code utility and type in the book order number, and the utility generates the bar code.

Title page: The title page is typically a duplicate of the front cover, but with certain elements omitted. Typically omitted are the artwork, company or product logos, and slogans. Some technical publications omit the title page altogether because of the seemingly needless duplication.

Edition notice: The edition notice is typically the first instance of regular text in a technical publication, although it is typically in smaller type. It occurs on the backside of the title page. If the technical publisher is taking the lean-and-mean approach and eliminating the title page, the edition notice will appear on the backside of the front cover. No one likes to read fine print, but take a look at the statements typically included in an edition notice:

— *Date of publication*: Included not only is the year but sometimes even the month that the book was published.

— *Edition number*: Whether the book is a first, second, or third edition.

— *Product applicability*: The edition notice typically indicates which platform, version, and release number of the product the book applies to.

— *Full title of the book*: Shown in italics.

— *Disclaimers*: Shockingly, product manufacturers will make statements to the effect that they do not guarantee the book is technically correct, complete, or free from writing problems or that the product is free from minor flaws or that it meets the needs of the customer. You'll be able to find additional disclaimers beyond these as well.

— *Copyright symbol and statement*: You'll see the circle-C copyright symbol and some statement warning readers not to copy the book without permission.

— *Copyright permissions*: The high-tech world often moves so rapidly that instead of creating their own versions of a product component and its corresponding documentation, companies will simply buy the code or design and the rights to reprint the documentation as well. This usually entails copyright acknowledgement in the edition notice (although if a lot of borrowing has happened, publishers must get creative about where to put all these acknowledgements).

— *Reader responses*: Sometimes, the edition notice will include some encouragement to customers to contact the company about product or documentation concerns. Instructions on how to contact the company are sometimes included in the edition notice. Included also is often a rather unfriendly statement that any customer communication becomes the property of the company.

— *Trademarks*: Some technical publications list known trademarks in the edition notice. This includes both the company's own trademarks and the trademarks of other companies referenced in the book. With the explosion of new products in the high-tech world, and thus the explosion of trademarks, some publications essentially throw up their hands and insert a simple statement that any references to trademarked product names are owned by their respective companies.

Disclaimers: See the section on edition notices, where disclaimers are usually tucked away. If a product or its publication needs a whole separate page for its disclaimers, I'm not buying it!

Trademarks: Although many companies do list their own and other companies' trademarks in the edition notice, some prefer to list them on a separate page, just after the edition notice. These placement decisions are almost strictly the province of company attorneys; as a writer, you may have to comply no matter how bad the the decision is in terms of book design or writing style.

Remember, you list only those trademarked product names that occur in that particular book. You'll notice that some publications go to extreme measures with trademarks: they'll asterisk or footnote the first, or even every occurrence of a trademarked product name. But again, these are directives of company attorneys unto which technical writers must resign themselves, however sadly.

Warranties: More legal stuff. These are the "guarantees" that the company will support concerning its product. Sometimes these are published in the front matter of the book; but, more appropriately from a book-design standpoint, they are printed on a separate card and inserted in the shrinkwrap of the book or the product. Again, as with edition notices, this is text you simply bring in as "boilerplate" and position in the right place within the book. However, you should be aware that companies sometimes maintain multiple versions of edition notices, safety notices, warranties, communication statements and other such.

As a writer, you must make sure that you are using the right version. And whatever you do, don't change the text of these boilerplate items, however horribly they are written. Changes typically must be approved by company attorneys.

Safety notices: Hardware products typically have a section of safety notices at the front of their books. These may occur as a subsection of the preface, for example, or as a separate section in their own right. These sections typically bring together all of the danger, warning, and caution notices that occur throughout the book and arrange them in some sort of logical way. But even with this up-front alert, hardware books still place the individual notices at the points where they apply.

Communication statements: Hardware books also require communications statements as stipulated by the governments of the countries to which these products are shipped. In the U.S., the FCC requires certain communications statements depending on the "class" of the hardware product. As a writer, you must be careful to use the right communication statement for the product you are documenting-and not to edit the statement in any way.

Table of contents: The table of contents usually contains at least a second level of detail so that readers can find what they need more precisely. Writers, editors, and book designers typically argue about the sequencing of the TOC. In terms of usability, it's much better to have the TOC as close to the front of the book as possible, if not at the very first of the book. In terms of legalities, however, people worry that all those communication statements, warranties, copyrights, trademarks, and safety notices should come first. In those places where usability wins out, books use every tactic they can to get this legalistic material out of the front matter: warranties are put on separate cards and shrink-wrapped with the book or product; warranties, communication statements, trademarks and other such may be dumped in appendixes.

List of figures: Technical manuals for ordinary users typically don't have lists of figures. In fact, the figures themselves typically do not have full-blown figure titles. But this isn't to say that a list of figures has no place in technical manuals. It all depends on the reader and the reader's needs-and the content of the book as well. If the book contains tables, illustrations, charts, graphs, and other such that readers will want to find directly, the figure list is order.

Preface: The function of the preface is to get readers ready to read the book. It does so by characterizing the content and purpose of the book, identifying or even briefly describing the product the book supports, explaining the type of reader for whom the book is meant, outlining the main contents of the book, showing any special conventions or terminology used in the book, providing support and marketing numbers, and other such. In traditional book publishing, the preface comes before the table of contents; but as discussed previously in the table of contents section, technical publishing people want the TOC to come earlier in the book for usability reasons.

Body chapters: Oh yes, and there is actual text in these books-it isn't all front matter! Little else to say here other than most technical books have chapters or sections, and, in some cases, parts. See the chapter on page design for format, style, and design issues for elements such as headers, footers, headings, lists, notices, tables, graphics, cross-references, and highlighting.

Appendixes: As you know, appendixes are for material that just doesn't seem to fit in the main part of a book but can't be left out of the book either. Appendixes are often the place for big unwieldy tables. Some technical publications have things like warranties in the appendixes. In terms of format, an appendix is just like a chapter-except that it is named "Appendix A" or some such, and the headers and footers match that different numbering and naming convention (A-1, A-2, and so on for pages in Appendix A).

Glossary: Some technical publications include a section of specialized terms and their definitions. Notice that most glossaries use a two-column layout. Typically the term and its definition make up a separate paragraph, with the term lowercase (unless it is a proper name) and in bold, followed by a period, then the definition in regular roman. Notice too that definitions are typically not complete sentences. Good glossary definitions should use the formal-sentence definition technique as described in the definition chapter of this online text. Multiple definitions are typically identified by arabic numbers in parentheses. Glossary paragraphs also contain See references to preferred terms and See also references to related terms.

Index: Indexes are also typically two-column and also contain See references to preferred terms and See also references to related terms.

Reader-response form: Some technical publications contain a mechanism to enable readers to send in comments, questions, and evaluation of the book. Of course, it turns out that these forms more often elicit complaints about faulty function in the product that the book documents. With the rise of the Internet, these forms have gone online, and books merely point to their location online.

Book design and layout: Typically, user guides and manuals produced by hardware and software manufacturers are designed in a rather austere and spartan way. High-tech companies develop new versions and releases of their product sometimes every nine months. Here sophisticated design is just not practical. Here are some of the typical layout and design features you'll see:

— Page size is often determined by packaging considerations as well as by standard page sizes available with printing companies. When page size is not a constraint, some companies will use the 8.5 × 11-inch page size-this makes production much easier for writers.

— Pages are typically designed with alternating right and left pages. The footer for the left (even) page includes the title of the book and the page number. The footer for the right (odd) page includes the title of the chapter.

— Practice is mixed on whether page numbering is consecutive throughout the book or by-chapter.

— Unless pages are rather small, the hanging-head design of headings in relation to pages is quite common in technical manuals. The hanging indent is usually one inch to one-and-a-half inches.

— Fonts are often 12-point Times New Roman for body text and Arial for headings. Standard line spacing and word spacing are used. See the chapter on highlighting for other typographical issues.

— Margins are fairly standard, one to two inches all the way around. Typically, an extra half-inch is used on inside margins to allow for binding.

— Typically, color is not used in these manuals and guides, usually out of cost and efficiency considerations.

9

Lists

Lists are useful because they emphasize certain information in regular text. When you see a list of three or four items strung out vertically on the page, rather than in normal paragraph format, you naturally notice it more and are likely to pay more attention to it. Certain types of lists also make for easier reading. For example, in instructions, it is a big help for each step to be numbered and separate from the preceding or following steps.

Lists also create more white space and spread out the text so that pages don't seem like solid walls of words. Like headings, the various types of lists are an important feature of professional technical writing: they help readers understand, remember, and review key points; they help readers follow a sequence of actions or events; and they break up long stretches of straight text.

Guidelines for Lists

Some general guidelines are given below:

— Use lists to highlight or emphasize text or to enumerate or make for easier reference.

— Make list items parallel in phrasing.

— Make sure that each item in the list reads grammatically with the lead-in.

— Use a lead-in to introduce the list items, to indicate the meaning or purpose of the list (and punctuate it with a colon).

— Never use headings as lead-ins for lists.

— Avoid overusing lists; using too many lists destroys their effectiveness.

— Use similar types of lists consistently in similar text in the same document.

Guidelines for Specific Types of Lists: It's difficult to state guidelines on choosing between the various kinds of lists, but here's a stab at it:

— Most importantly, use numbered lists for items that are in a required order (such as step-by-step instructions) or for items that must be referred to by item number. Use bulleted lists for items that are in no required order.

— With in-sentence lists, there are no conventions when to use letters (a), (b), and so on, as opposed to numbers (1), (2), and so on. If you are in a numbered list and need a sublist, use letters, to contrast with the numbers. Otherwise, there really seem to be no widely agreed-upon guidelines--just be consistent!

— Use vertical lists as opposed to in-sentence lists when you want the emphasis provided by the vertical presentation. In-sentence lists provide only minimal emphasis; vertical lists provide much more.

— Avoid using in-sentence lists when there are more than 4 or 5 items; use a vertical format instead.

— Within an individual report, use in-sentence lists and vertical lists consistently for similar situations. For example, if you have topic overviews for each section of a report, use in-sentence or vertical lists for the overview--but don't mix them for that particular use.

Problems with Lists

Problems with lists usually include the following:

— Mix-up between numbered and bulleted lists

— Lack of parallel phrasing in the list items

— Use of single parentheses on the list-item number or letter

— Run-over lines not aligned with the text of list items

— Lack of a strong lead-in sentence introducing list items, and lack of a colon to punctuation lead-ins

— Inconsistent caps style in list items

— Unnecessary punctuation of list items

— Inconsistent use of lists in similar text

— Lists that have too many items and need to be subdivided or consolidated

Format for Lists

Use the following for specific details on the capitalization, typography (bold, underlining, different fonts, different types sizes), and spacing for each type of list.

In-sentence lists: Use these guidelines for in-sentence lists:

1. Use a colon to introduce the list items only if a complete sentence precedes the list. In this problem version, the colon breaks right into the middle of a sentence:

   Problem: For this project, you need: tape, scissors, and white-out.

   Revision: For this project, you need tape, scissors, and white-out.

2. Use both opening and closing parentheses on the list item numbers or letters: (a) item, (b) item, etc.

3. Use either regular Arabic numbers or lowercase letters within the parentheses, but use them consistently. (Do not

punctuate either with periods). Use lowercase for the text of in-sentence lists items, except when regular capitalization rules require caps.

4. Punctuate the list items with commas if they are not complete sentences; with semicolons, if they are complete sentences.

5. Use the same spacing for in-sentence lists as in regular non-list text.

6. Whenever possible, make the in-sentence list occur at the end of the sentence. Never place an in-sentence list introduced by a colon anywhere but at the end of the sentence, as in this example:

   Problem: The following items: tape, scissors, and white-out are needed for this project.

   Revision: The following items are needed for this project: tape, scissors, and white-out.

Simple vertical lists: Use these guidelines for simple vertical lists:

1. Introduce the list with a lead-in sentence (the lead-in need not be a complete sentence; the list items can complete the lead-in). Punctuate the lead-in with a colon.

2. Use simple vertical lists when the list items do not need to be emphasized, and are listed vertically merely for ease of reading.

3. Use sentence-style capitalization on list items.

4. Begin run-over lines under the text of the list item, not the regular left margin; singlespace list items that are two to three lines long (but use doublespace for lengthy list items).

5. Use regular doublespacing between the surrounding text and the list; doublespace between list items.

6. Indent the list items 3 to 5 spaces (start the item on the third or fifth column).

7. Punctuate list items only if they are complete sentences or verb phrases that complete the sentence begun by the lead-in (and use periods in these two cases).
8. Watch out for lists with more than 6 or 8 list items; for long lists, look for ways to subdivide or consolidate. Avoid single-item lists.
9. When possible, omit articles (a, an, the) from the beginning of list items.

Bulleted vertical lists: Use these guidelines for bulleted vertical lists:

1. Introduce the list with a lead-in sentence (the lead-in need not be a complete sentence; the list items can complete the lead-in). Punctuate the lead-in sentence with a colon.
2. Use bulleted lists when the list items are in no necessary order and when you want to emphasize the items in the list.
3. Use asterisks or hyphens if you have no access to an actual bullet.
4. Use sentence-style capitalization on list items.
5. Begin run-over lines under the text of the list item, not the bullet; singlespace list items that are two to three lines long (but use doublespace for lengthy list items).
6. Use regular doublespacing between the surrounding text and the bulleted list; doublespace between list items.
7. Indent the list items 3 to 5 spaces (start the bullet on the third or fifth column). Leave 1 space between the bullet and the start of the list item.
8. Punctuate bulleted list items only if they are complete sentences or verb phrases that complete the sentence begun by the lead-in (and use periods in these two cases).
9. Watch out for bulleted lists with more than 6 or 8 list items; for long bulleted lists, look for ways to subdivide or consolidate. Avoid single-item bulleted lists.

10. When possible, omit articles (a, an, the) from the beginning of list items.

Numbered vertical lists: Use these guidelines for numbered vertical lists:

1. Introduce the list with a lead-in sentence (the lead-in need not be a complete sentence; the list items can complete the lead-in). Punctuate the lead-in sentence with a colon.

2. Use numbered lists when the list items are in a required order (for example, chronological).

3. Type the number followed by a period; do not use parentheses on the number.

4. Use sentence-style capitalization on list items.

5. Begin run-over lines under the text of the list item, not the number; singlespace list items that are two to three lines long (but use doublespace for lengthy list items).

6. Use regular doublespacing between the surrounding text and the numbered list; doublespace between list items.

7. Indent the list items 3 to 5 spaces (start the number on the third or fifth column). Leave 1 space between the period after the number and the start of the list item.

8. Punctuate numbered list items only if they are complete sentences or verb phrases that complete the sentence begun by the lead-in (and use periods in these two cases).

9. Watch out for numbered lists with more than 8 or 10 list items; for long numbered lists, look for ways to subdivide or consolidate. Avoid single-item numbered lists.

10. When possible, omit articles (a, an, the) from the beginning of list items.

Two-column lists: Use these guidelines for two-column lists:

1. Use two-column lists when you have a series of paired items, for example, terms and definitions.

2. Introduce the list with a lead-in sentence that is a complete sentence. Punctuate the lead-in sentence with a colon.

3. Column headings are optional; if used, align them to the left margin of the text of the columns.

4. Indent the left column 3 to 5 spaces; leave at least 3 spaces between the right margin of the left column and the left margin of the right column.

5. Use sentence-style capitalization for both columns.

6. Punctuate items in the columns only if they are complete sentences.

7. Doublespace between the list items; but singlespace within the items.

8. Left-align both columns.

9. When possible, omit articles (a, an, the) from the beginning of list items.

Lists with run-in headings: One last little variation on lists is the vertical list with run-in headings or labels at the beginning of the items. This format is used extensively in this book. It's like another way of doing a two-column list. Two-column lists can be difficult--you have to get the spacing right between the two columns and reformat every run-over line in the second column. You can use bold or italics for the actual run-in heading.

Single spaced Text: For singlespaced text, use your document-design "eye" to decide on spacing. Leave either one or two blank lines between running text and lists--depending on what looks best to you. One area that is wide open for individual judgment is whether to add space between vertical list items (loose format) or to keep them singlespaced (compact format). Again, use your document-design eye on this. If the items are several lines each and if there are numerous items, the loose format may be more readable.

10

Special Notices

Special notices are an important feature of professional technical writing: they highlight special information readers need to know to understand what they are reading, to accomplish what they want to do, to prevent damage to equipment, and to keep from hurting themselves or others.

Guidelines for Notices

Guidelines in planning and designing special notices

1. Use special notices to emphasize key points or warn or caution readers about damage or injury.

2. Be careful to use the types of special notices precisely, for their defined purposes. Use the four types of special notices in the following ways:

   — Note-To emphasize points or remind readers of something, or to indicate minor problems in the outcome of what they are doing.

   — Warning -To warn readers about the possibility of minor injury to themselves or others.

   — Caution -To warn readers about possible damage to equipment or data or about potential problems in the outcome of what they are doing.

— Danger-To warn readers about the possibility of serious or fatal injury to themselves or others.

Deciding on which type of notice to use is not an exact science. Don't use a danger notice when a warning is more appropriate. Also, use notices in a consistent way throughout a report. Do not create your own notices, such as putting "Important:" in place of "Warning."

1. Place special notices at the point in text where they are needed. For example, place a caution or danger notice before discussing a step in which readers might hurt themselves.

2. Avoid having too many special notices at any one point in the text. Otherwise, the effectiveness of their special format will be lost.

3. With warnings, cautions, and danger notices, explain the consequences of not paying attention to the notice. State what will happen if the reader does not heed the notice.

4. The following examples use bold. If you have no access to bold, use underlines instead. Avoid all-caps for the text of any special notice.

Format for Special Notices

Use the following for specific details on the capitalization, typography (bold, underlining, different fonts, different types sizes), and spacing for each type of special notice:

Use the following format for simple notes

1. Type the word "Note" followed by a colon. (Underline the word, or use bold if you have it.)

2. Begin typing the text of the note one space after the colon. (But don't put the text of the note in bold.)

3. Singlespace within the text of the note; skip one line above and below the note.

4. Start run-over lines on the regular left margin.
5. Align the note with the text to which it refers.

Use the following format for multiple notes:

1. Type the word "Notes" followed by a colon. (Underline the word, or use bold if you have it.)
2. Use a numbered list for the individual notes; in it, follow the rules for numbered lists. (Do not use bold for the individual notes.)
3. Align the notes with the text to which the refer; skip one line above and below the notes.
4. Use this format when you have so many notes that they would distracting to present individually.

Warning: Use the following format for warnings:

1. Type the word "Warning," follow with a colon, italicize.
2. Tab to begin the text of the warning. (Try for 0.25 to 0.5 inches of space between the end of the warning label and the beginning of the text.)
3. Use regular body font for the text of the warning notice (no bold, no italics, no all-caps, no color).
4. Align the warning notice with the text it refers to.
5. Singlespace the text of the notice notice; skip one line above and below the caution notice.

Example of a warning notice. Use this one to alert readers to the possibility of minor injury.

Caution: Use the following format for caution notices:

1. Type the word "Caution" follow it with a colon, and bold both the label and the colon.
2. Skip one line and begin the text of the caution aligned with the start of the caution label.

3. Singlespace the text of the caution; skip one line above and below the notice.

4. Align the caution notice with the text it refers to (in the preceding, the warning notice occurs within a numbered list and is indented accordingly).

Danger: Use the following format for danger notices:

1. Type the word "DANGER" in all-caps. (Underline it, or use bold.)

2. Align the danger notice with the text it refers to.

3. Singlespace the text of the danger notice; skip one line above and below the danger notice.

4. Use bold on the text of the danger notice if you have it (but never all-caps).

5. If you have graphics capability, draw a box around the danger notice (including the label).

Danger notice. Use this one to alert readers of the possibility of serious injury or fatality.

Other formatting issues

Special Alignment: Special notices must align to the text to which they refer. For example, if you have a note that adds some special detail to something in a bulleted list item, you must align that note to the text of the bulleted item. Of course, if the note follows a bulleted list but refers to the whole list, then you can use the regular left margin.

Singlespaced Text: All of the examples and discussion in this unit are based on doublespaced text. For singlespaced text, use your document-design "eye" to decide on spacing. Leave either one blank lines between running text and special notices-depending on what looks best to you. (And of course both running text and the text of the special notices would be singlespaced.)

Placement of Special Notices. The standard rule is to place special notices before the point at which they are relevant. For example, you warn readers to back up all data before you tell them to reformat their hard drive. However, in practice this applies to serious special notices where great harm to data, equipment, or people is likely to ensue.

One technique used by very cautious writers (maybe those who have been burned) is to place all serious notices (warnings, cautions, and dangers) somewhere at the beginning of the document, and then repeat them individually where they apply.

Multiple Special Notices: You run into situations where you have three or four special notices, all jammed together in the same part of the text, each one following another. This is a problem because the whole point of the special formatting of the notices is lost: something is special because it is different from the surrounding. The solution to this problem is to create one identifying heading (for example, "Notes and Warnings"), and then list the notices (either bulleted or numbered) below it.

11

Graphics and Tables

A lot of professional, technical writing contains graphics - drawings, diagrams, photographs, illustrations of all sorts, tables, pie charts, bar charts, line graphs, flow charts, and so on. Once you get the hang of putting graphics like these into your writing, you should consider yourself obligated to use graphics whenever the situation naturally would call for them. Unlike what you might fear, producing graphics is not such a terrible task - in fact, it can be fun. You don't have to be a professional graphics artist or technical draftsperson to produce graphics for your technical writing. There are ways to produce professional-looking graphics with tape, scissors, white-out, and a decent photocopying machine.

Graphics

You can use graphics to represent the following elements in your technical writing:

— *Objects*: If you're describing a fuel-injection system, you'll probably need a drawing or diagram of the thing. If you are explaining how to graft a fruit tree, you'll need some illustrations of how that task is done. Photographs, drawings, diagrams, and schematics are the types of graphics that show objects.

— *Numbers*: If you're discussing the rising cost of housing in Austin, you could use a table with the columns being for five-year periods since 1970; the rows could be for different types of housing. You could show the same data in the form of bar charts, pie charts, or line graphs. Tables, bar charts, pie charts, and line graphs are some of the principal ways to show numerical data.

— *Concepts*: If you want to show how your company is organized, the relationships of the different departments and officials, you could set up an organization chart-boxes and circles connected with lines that show how everything is hierarchically arranged and related. This would be an example of a graphic for a concept: this type depicts nonphysical, conceptual things and their relationships.

— *Words*: And finally graphics are used to depict words. You've probably noticed how textbooks put key definitions in a box, maybe with different color. The same can be done with key points or extended examples. Not the sexiest form of graphics, but it still qualifies, and it's good to keep in mind as a useful technique in certain situations.

Drawings, Diagrams, Photos

In the realm of illustrations and photographs, the types run from minimal detail to maximal. A simple line drawing of how to graft a fruit tree reduces the detail to simple lines representing the hands, the tools, the graft stock, and graft. Diagrams are a more abstract, schematic view of things, for example, a wiring diagram of a clock radio; it hardly resembles the actual physical thing at all. And of course photographs provide the most detail of all. These graphics, supplying gradations of detail as they do, have their varying uses. Here are some examples:

— In instructions, simple drawings (often called line drawings because they use just lines, without other detail such as shading) are the most common. They simplify the situation and the objects so that the reader can focus on the key details.

— In descriptions, you would want to use drawings, but in this case drawings with more detail, such as shading and depth perspectives.

— In feasibility, recommendation, and evaluation reports, photographs are often used. For example, if you are recommending a photocopier, you might want to include photos of the leading contenders.

Formatting requirements: When you use an illustration in a report, there are several requirements to keep in mind:

— *Labels*: Just about any illustration should contain labels - words and phrases - with pointers to the parts of the things being depicted.

— *Keys*: If the illustration has certain shadings, colors, line styles, or other such details that have a special meaning in the illustration, these should be indicated in a key - an area in an unused corner of the illustration that deciphers their meaning.

— *Titles*: Except in special cases, illustrations should have titles, and these titles should be numbered (Figure 1, Figure 2, and so on). The exceptions are these: if you have lots of illustrations (for example, in certain instructions, there are illustrations practically after every paragraph) and if there is no benefit from the titles; if you only have one or two illustrations and they are not cross-referenced; if you do not cross-reference your illustrations. In some of these cases, you might want to keep the title but discard the word "Figure" and the number following it.

— *Cross-references*: Almost all illustrations should be referred to from the relevant point in the discussion.

— *Location within the report* - Ideally, you place illustrations just after the point where they are needed. However, sometimes because of the pagination (the way the text falls on the pages) and the size of the illustrations, this close placement is not possible. No problem - just put the illustration at the top of the next page; that is what the figure-numbering system is for.

— *Size of illustrations*: Again, ideally, you want illustrations to be between one-half to one-quarter of the vertical size of the page. You want them to fit on the page with other text. In fact, that's what you really want - to interperse text and graphics in a report. What you do not want is to append the illustration to the back of the report! When you have a large illustration, use a photocopier to reduce it.

— *Placement within margins*: Make sure that your illustrations fit neatly and comfortably within standard margins. You don't want the illustration spilling over into the right or left margins. You want to allow the equivalent of at least 2 blank lines above and below the illustration.

— Level of technical detail: And, rather obviously, you want illustrations to be at the right technical level for your readers. No chip circuitry diagrams for computer beginners!

Producing illustrations: There are several options to create a graphics: photocopying, scanning, clip art, and hand-drawing. (And now most mainstream word-processing applications enable you to generate various kinds of graphs and charts, not to mention graphics and business software.) In all of these production methods, don't forget that you must indicate the source of the borrowed graphic.

— Photocopying is the easiest solution to creating graphics - and it's legal (if you do it right)! Find the illustrations that you want, make good high-quality photocopies of them, trim off the figure titles and other unnecessary or inappropriate textual material (leave the labels and keys), and then leave space in your own document so that the trimmed photocopy will fit with at least 2 blank lines above and below it. Remember to reduce or enlarge the copy so that it fits nicely on the page. Also remember that ideal graphics are one-half to one-quarter the size of the page. Intersperse graphics with text! When you make the final copy of your document, tape in the copied graphics, photocopy the entire document, and hand in the photocopy (not the original).

— Scanning is a neat way to pull graphics into your document files. You don't have to tape them to a copy then photocopy the document - they are there, fully integrated. However, there are some pretty cheap scanners that produce blurry, low-quality images. They're adequate for our technical writing course, but not for serious professional work.

— Lots of clip art is becoming available with software programs and on the Internet. For fairly common objects such as computers, telephones, and such, you can insert these into your document and add labels to them.

— Hand-drawing may not be as out of the question as you might think. Take a blank sheet of paper and start sketching lightly with a soft-leaded pencil. Keep working until you have the drawing the way you like. Then use a black marker to ink in the lines that you want, and erase the stray pencil markings. Now, treat this drawing the way you would any photocopied image. Cut it out, tape it in your document, photocopy it as well as all other pages, then hand in the photocopy.

Photographs

At least as the way things stand right now in the 1990s, getting photographs into reports is a problem. They don't photocopy well (although they do better now than just a few years ago). They don't attach to report pages very well either. High-quality scanning equipment may be the better alternative in this area, although a scanned image costs $5 to $10 right now at local copy shops equipped to offer this service. If you need to use photographs in your technical reports for a technical writing course, consult with your instructor. After all, these are writing courses, not graphic arts courses - taped-in or photocopied photographs may be okay in this setting.

Tables

Tables, of course, are those rows and columns of numbers and words, mostly numbers. They permit rapid access to and relatively easy comparison of information. If the data is arranged chronologically (for example, sales figures over a ten-year period), the table can show trends - patterns of rising or falling activity. Of course, tables are not necessarily the most vivid or dramatic means of showing such trends or relationships between data - that's why we have charts and graphs.

Uses for Tables

The biggest use of tables is for numerical data. Imagine that you are comparing different models of laser printers in terms of physical characteristics such as height, depth, length, weight, and so on - perfect for a table. However, don't get locked into the notion that tables are strictly for numerical data. Whenever you have situations where you discuss several things about which you provide the same categories of detail, you've got a possibility for a table.

For example, imagine that you were comparing several models of a laser printer: you'd be saying the same category of thing about each printer (its cost, print speed, supply costs, warranty terms, and so on). This is ideal stuff for a table, and it would be mostly words rather than numbers (and in this case, you'd probably want to leave the textual discussion where it is and "re-present" the information in table form.

Table format

In its simplest form, a table is a group of rows and columns of data. At the top of each column is a column heading, which defines or identifies the contents of that column (and often it indicates the unit of measurement). On the left edge of the table may be row headings, which define or identify the contents of that row. Things get tricky when rows or columns must be grouped or subdivided. In such cases, you have to create row or column subheadings.

Traditionally, the title of a table is placed on top of the table or is the first row of the table. If the contents of the table are obvious and there is no need to cross-reference the table from anywhere else in the report, you can omit the title. To make life simpler, you can consider tables as figures (the same as illustrations and other graphics), and number them within the same sequence. As for specific style and formatting guidelines for tables, keep these in mind:

— Refer to the table in the text just preceding the table. Explain the general significance of the data in the table; don't expect readers to figure it out entirely for themselves.

— Don't overwhelm readers with monster 11-column, 30-row tables! Simplify the table data down to just that amount of data that illustrates your point - without of course distorting that data.

— Don't put the word or abbreviation for the unit of measurement in every cell of a column. For example, in a column of measurements all in millimeters, don't put "mm" after every number. Put the abbreviation in parentheses in the column or row heading.

— Right- or decimal-align numbers in the columns. If the 123 and 4 were in a column, the 4 would be right below the 3, not the 1.

— Normally, words in columns are left-justified.

— Column headings are centered over the columns of numerical data (forming a T-shape); left-aligned with columns of text. The alignment of column headings to the actual columnar data is variable. If you have a column of two- or three-letter words, you'd probably want to center the column heading over that data, even those it is words not numbers.

— When there is some special point you need to make about one or more of the items in the table, use a footnote instead of clogging up the table with the information.

Producing tables: Normally, you'll be borrowing information in which a good table occurs. If it's a simple table without too many rows and columns, retype it yourself into your own document (but remember to document where you borrowed it from in the figure title). However, if it is a big table with lots of data, you're justified in photopcopying it and bringing it into your report that way. When you manually type tables, consider putting a string of hyphens between the column headings and the first row of data and another string of hyphens between the last row of data and any totals the table has.

Most of the advanced word-processing software packages, such as Word and WordPerfect, now have table-generating tools. You don't have to draw the lines and other formatting details. Occasionally, in rough-draft technical reports, information is presented in regular running-text form that could be better presented in table (or tabular) form. Be sure and look back over your rough drafts for material that can transformed into tables.

Charts and graphs

Charts and graphs are actually just another way of presenting the same data that is presented in tables - although a more dramatic and interesting one. At the same time, however, you get less detail or less precision in a chart or diagram than you do in the table. Imagine the difference between a table of sales figures for a ten-year period and a line graph for that same data. You get a better sense of the overall trend in the graph but not the precise dollar amount.

Formatting requirements: When you create charts and diagrams, keep these requirements in mind:

— *Axis labels*: In bar charts and line graphs, don't forget to indicate what the x and y axes represent. One axis might indicate millions of dollars; the other, five-year segments from 1960 to the present.

— *Keys*: Bar charts, line graphs, and pie charts often use special color, shading, or line style (solid or dashed). Be sure to indicate what these mean; translate them in a key (a box) in some unused place in the chart or graph.

— *Figure titles*: For most charts and graphs, you'll want to include a title, in many cases, a numbered title. Readers need some way of knowing what they are looking at. And don't forget to cite the source of any information you borrowed in order to create the graphic. The standard rule for when to number figures or tables is this: if you cross-reference the figure or table elsewhere in the text.

— *Cross-references*: Whenever you use a chart or graph, don't forget to put a cross-reference to it from the related text. With that cross-reference, provide some explanation of what is going on in the graphic, how to interpret it, what its basic trends are, and so on.

— *Documentation*: When you borrow information to create a graphic, be sure to use the standard format to indicate the source. It does not matter whether you photocopy the graphic and tape it into your report, retype the graphic (for example, a table), trace or draw the graphic freehand, or take some subset of the data (for example, using data from a table to create a bar chart) - it is all borrowed information, which some brave and noble soul worked hard to develop and who deserves credit for that effort.

Producing charts and graphs: As with illustrations, you have these options for creating charts and graphs: photocopying from other sources, generating your own with special software, and manual creating your own. Many of the text-processing software packages have fancy features for generating charts and graphs - you just crank in your data, specify the format you want, and let 'er rip.

Documenting Graphics

It's perfectly legal to borrow graphics - to trace, photocopy, scan, or extract subsets of data from them. But you're obligated to cite your sources for graphics just as you are for the words you borrow. General guidelines for graphics - a review. The preceding sections repeat a number of common guidelines that need to be stated all in one place. These are important!

— Use graphics whenever they would normally be necessary - don't wimp out because it seems like too much trouble! But at the same time, don't get hung up about creating perfect graphics (photocopies work just fine for our purposes as long as you cite your source). This course is a writing course, not a graphic-arts course.

— Always discuss graphics in nearby text preceding the graphic. Don't just throw a graphic out there unexplained. Orient readers to the graphic; explain its basic meaning.

— If a certain graphic is difficult to produce, discuss the problem with your instructor (you might be able to leave a blank with a descriptive note in the middle).

— Make sure your graphics are appropriate to your audience, subject matter, and purpose - don't zap beginners with advanced, highly technical graphics they can't understand.

— Intersperse graphics and text on the same page. Don't put graphics on pages by themselves; don't attach them to the end of documents.

— Use figure titles for graphics (only a few exceptions to this rule).

— Indicate the source of any graphic you have borrowed - this includes tables, illustrations, charts, and graphs. Whenever you borrow a graphic from some other source, document that fact in the figure title.

— Include identifying detail such as illustration labels, axis labels, keys, and so on. But don't hand-write them in - use the labels from the original photocopy or type them.

— Make sure graphics fit within normal margins - if they don't, enlarge or reduce the copies. Leave at least 2 blank lines above and below graphics.

— When you tape graphics in to your report, photocopy your entire report, not just the pages on which the tape-ins occur. Hand in the entire photocopied document, not the original and not a mixture of original and photocopied pages.

— Don't manually add color or other detail on the pages of the final copy that you intend to submit - in other words, don't draw on the final copy. Any details like these should be added before photocopying. If you must have color, use color photocopying equipment.

— Place graphics as near to the point in the text where they are relevant as is reasonable. However, if a graphic does not fit properly on one page, put it at the top of the next, and continue with regular text on the preceding page.

Don't leave half a page blank just to keep a graphic near the text it is associated with.

— Except for graphics that need no figure title, cross-reference all graphics from the appropriate text. In the cross-reference, give the figure number (figure title and page are optional), indicate the subject matter of the graphic, and provide explanatory information as necessary.

12

Highlighting and Emphasis

Highlighting Problems

Actually, several problems involving emphasis can occur:

— *Overkill*: Emphasis techniques can be used in excess---the text swarms with a dizzying array of bold, italics, alternate fonts, caps, color.

— *Inconsistency*: Emphasis techniques can also be used inconsistently, which sends conflicting, confusing messages to readers.

— *Illogical function*: Emphasis techniques can also not be in keeping with readers' needs. Writers may choose the wrong things to emphasize and fail to emphasize the right things.

Using point of emphasis techniques: Used properly, they highlight text that readers must see, for example, alerting them to actions they must take or avoid. Emphasis techniques can make following a procedure considerably easier. But the design of the highlighting scheme (which organizes the emphasis techniques around a system of use) must be based on the reader, the tasks that the reader must accomplish, and the characteristics of the text (or the technology) that the reader is using.

Highlighting Fundamentals

Consider a few fundamental principles of emphasis:

— Practically anything that is different from regular body text can function as an emphasis technique.

— Things like italics, bold, underscores, caps, different size type, alternate fonts, color, the various graphical ingenuities (showing, reverse color, outline fonts) can act as emphasis techniques.

— Used in excess, any emphasis technique or combination of emphasis techniques can lose their ability to emphasize and become busy and distracting.

— Used in excess, any emphasis technique or combination of emphasis techniques can cause readers to be reluctant to read a text, if not avoid it altogether.

— When extended text must be emphasized, use the special-notice format (rather creating all-bold or all-caps paragraphs, for example).

— A carefully planned functional relationship must exist between the text that is emphasized and the emphasis technique that is used.

— Emphasis techniques must be used consistently to prevent readers from becoming confused.

— To promote consistency, you must use a style guide or style sheet, which records all of your decisions about how you are going to use emphasis techniques.

— To help your readers understand your highlighting scheme, you must include a brief section somewhere in your document (usually in the preface) explaining how you're going to be using the emphasis techniques.

Your readers need to be informed as to the highlighting scheme you plan to use. This can be handled in the preface: include a section called "Highlighting" or "Typographical

Conventions" where you list how you use italics, bold, fonts, and other such effects.

Emphasis Techniques

Bold: In publishing, technical publishing in particular, usage is mixed as to whether to use bold or italics for basic emphasis. For example, if you want to emphasize that readers should not turn off the computer without first shutting it down, the "not" can be bold or italics. Traditionally, italics has been used, but, perhaps because of computers, bold is commonly used as well. Whichever technique you use, use it consistently throughout your text or library of related texts.

By the way, readers are not likely to be able to distinguish between levels of emphasis: for example, using italics for important text and bold for very important text is likely to be lost on most readers. If you are tempted to make an entire paragraph bold, remember one of the principle of emphasis discussed above: using too much of an emphasis technique causes the effect of the technique to be lost. Not only that, but too much emphasis makes readers less inclined to read. Instead of carefully reading an all-bold paragraph, readers may just ignore it entirely!

Instead of creating an all-bold paragraph, use the special-notice format. In it, a key word (for example, Important, Note, Danger, Caution, Warning) is bolded, while the rest of the text is left regular roman (that is, the same font and style as the regular body text). Legitimate use of bold in technical texts varies widely. As long as you develop a scheme that is directly related to the reader's need and to the characteristics of the text (or technology) and that does not lead to overkill, your use of bold should work fine. Here are some common, standard uses of bold:

— Simple emphasis. As discussed in the preceding, some technical texts use bold for simple emphasis instead of the traditional italics. For example, "Do not turn off the computer before shutting it down."

— Headings. Obviously, headings use bold in addition to other typographical effects such as different fonts, large type sizes, italics, and even color.

— Commands. Computer texts commonly use bold for commands, for example, "Use the move command to rename UNIX files." See the section on highlighting computer text for a review of the complete set of emphasis techniques.

— Buttons that initiate commands. In a graphical user interface, some of the buttons initiate commands. For example, "press the Exit button to exit the application."

— Field labels. While some computer text bolds field labels, it is not general practice because it leads to highlighting overkill. For example, "In the Indentation area of the dialog box, click on Left." More common is to use the cap style used on the screen. Though by no means standard, it's preferable to write this: "In the Indentation area of the dialog box, click on Left."

— Keyboard or mouse buttons. Another highlighting technique not commonly in practice is to bold the name of a keyboard key or mouse button. For example, "Press the Q key or the left mouse button."

— Information that readers supply. Some computer texts bold text that readers are to type in, but certainly not all. For example, "Type guest and press the Enter key." (The section on common highlighting schemes for computer text points out that an alternate font, typically Courier, is used for text that readers must type in: "Type guest and press the Enter key.")

— Information displayed on the equipment or screen. Some computer texts also bold messages that are displayed on the screen, for example, "The system will then display Do you want to continue?" Some texts also bold the code numbers and letters displayed in the digital read-out windows on computer hardware. For example, "As the computer boots up, the digital read-out window will display 8888." (Again, computer text commonly uses an alternate font such as Courier for system-displayed text.)

— Labels on hardware. Another practice that is not particularly common in computer publishing is to bold the name of a hardware label. For example, "Press the Reset button to reboot the computer."

— Lead-in labels in list items: When you have a long list of bulleted or numbered items, a nice touch is to create a lead-in labels for each item and either bold or italicize it. (The bulleted items you are currently looking at use italics for the lead-in labels because there is so much bold in the text already.)

— Labels on special notices: As mentioned earlier, special notices are the best technique for emphasizing extended text. If you have a sentence or short paragraph you want to emphasize, don't make it all bold---use a special notice instead. With special notices, typically only the Danger, Warning, Caution, Important, or Note label is bolded.

— Definitions in definition (two-column) lists: In a two-column list in which the terms to be defined are in the left column and the definitions of those terms are in the right column, it's common for the terms to be bolded. And of course, this practice extends to any two-column list, not just to those where terms are being defined.

— Labels in figures: It's fairly common for labels used within figures to be bolded: for example, the label On/Off switch would be bold with an arrow leading to the part of the figure depicting that switch.

— Table or figure titles: It's quite standard for the titles of tables and figures to be bold.

— Column headings in tables: Standard too is to bold table column headings. For example, if you had a table that compared autombile costs over a five-year period, the first column "Autombiles" would be bold. The column headings for each of the five years, for example, "1995," would also be bold. (Row headings are also bolded under certain conditions.

You'll notice that the preceding discussion stated no absolute rules. that's the way it is: technical publishing practice is quite varied. The main idea is to develop a logical, controlled system of highlighting, use it consistently, and document it in a style guide so that you and your documentation team members can refer to it.

Italics: Here are some of the standard uses for italics:

— Simple emphasis: As mentioned earlier, usage is mixed on whether to use bold or italics for simple emphasis, although italics has been traditionai: for example, "Do not turn off the computer before shutting it down." Whichever you use, be consistent with it, and document it in your style guide or style sheet so that everybody on your document team can see it. If you're not sure which to use, use italics for simple emphasis: it's less busy.

— Variables: In computer publishing, one of the most common uses of italics is for variables. For example: copy oldfile newfile

Users know not to type oldfile or newfile but to substitute their own file names instead.

— Table titles; row and column headings: Some table styles use italics instead of bold for table titles, row and column headings, or both. For some document designers, the look is cleaner, smoother, cooler to the eye.

— Special-notice labels: The "note" special notice uses italics for the label "Note." Warning, caution, and danger notices use varying styles of bold, however, to attract more attention.

— Figure titles and labels: You'll notice that some style use italics for figure titles, as opposed to bold. The choice is arbitrary, although italics is cooler and less busy to the eye. Similarly, you'll see labels -- those words within a figure naming and pointing to portions of the graphic -- using italics instead of bold.

— List lead-in headings: As already mentioned, when you have a long list of bulleted or numbered items, a nice touch is to create a lead-in labels for each item and either bold or italicize it. (The bulleted items you are currently looking at use italics for the lead-in labels.)

— Headings: In headings, italics is often used in combination with other effects such as bold, larger type sizes, or alternate fonts.

— Definitions in definition (two-column) lists: While bold is more common for the items in the left column of a two-column list, italics is also used.

Underscores: There is almost no reason for using underscores in technical text. In the days of typewritten text, there certainly was. However, in these times, when bold, italics and other such typographical effects are readily available, underscores look obsolete. If you want to emphasize something, use your standard guidelines -- for example, use italics or bold.

Don't try to create gradations of emphasis: for example, a scale of increasing importance ranging from italics to bold to underscore will be lost on your readers. If you see good use of underscores in technical text, it will probably occur in heading design.

Capitalization: In technical publishing, there seems to be a running battle between technical writers and technical experts over capitalization. Technical experts like to use initial caps for practically every component and process in a system, while technical writers insist on using caps for proper names only. Also, technical experts (and management) typically use all caps for text they consider important and want readers to attend to.

As a technical writer, hold the line against capitalization. Capital letters are distracting; all-caps text is uncomfortable to read. Capital letters create a busy text, which sends lots of unnecessary signals. Capital letters are traditionally intended for proper names such as Microsoft, Netscape, Gateway, Dell Computers, WordPerfect, Pagemaker, and so on. The classic guidelines in technical publishing is to capitalize the names of separately orderable products only.

However, the politics of organizations bends this guideline considerably. If a company is proud of a certain feature in its new release, for example, EnergyMiser, it will capitalize it, even though you can't order it separately. This is the point at which capitalization is being for emphasis. As a technical writer, you'll want to user caps for proper names and keep the use of caps as an emphasis technique to a minimum. Here are some typical guidelines for capitalization:

— Use the exact capitalization style of messages shown on the computer screen, menu or screen names, field names, hardware labels, and so on.

— Do not use capital letters for emphasis; use italics or bold instead.

— Do not use all-caps for any extended text; use the special-notice format instead.

— Do not capitalize the names of the components or processes of a product. Capitalize only the names of products, that is, components that are separately orderable.

For example, your product may be called WordStuff and of course it must be capitalized according to the style dictated bny the marketing and product planners. However, one WordStuff's features called "spell checker" shouldn't be capitalized—just about everybody has one of those. However, WordStuff may have a feature called "ZippyFormat" and other called "Image Worker." Even though these are not separately orderable, you will want to use the initial-cap style because of their specialstyle and the ir marketing value. "Image Worker" is obviously something WordStuff, Inc., wants to show off -- therefore, the caps.

Single or double quotation marks: Quotation marks are often mistakenly used as emphasis techniques in technical text. As a technical writer, limit quotation marks to the traditional usage, which includes quoted speech; numbers, letters, or words referred to as such. Quotation marks, like capital letters, tend to create a busy, distracting text and therefore should be avoided.

Well-designed computer text avoids quotation marks rather vigorously. One of the primary reasons is that some readers might mistakenly assume that they must include the quotation marks in the commands they enter.

Instead of	Use the "move" command.
Write	Use the move command.
Instead of	Enter "copy install installnow."
Write	Enter copy install installnow.

Note: While some technical texts have well-defined uses for single quotation marks, in general there is no standard use for single quotation marks, other than the traditional quotation-within-a-quotation rule. When you see single quotation marks within technical text, there is usually no more rationale for their use than there is for double quotation marks.

Alternate fonts: One of the most common styles in volving alternate fonts is to use Courier or some similar monospaced, old-typewriter-style font in contrast to the standard body font (such as Times New Roman or Helvetica). You can create this effect in web page by using the <KBD> tags. For example, "type install to install the program." Here's a review of the common uses of alternate fonts:

— Example text: To signal that an example rather than a required entry is being shown, an alternate font like Courier is often used: For example, if you want to copy a file, type "copy yourfile.txt myfile.txt" A file called myfile.txt will be created, and its contents will be the same as yourfile.txt.

— Displayed text: Computers and other equipment typically display things such as warning or status codes or error messages. These appear on monitor or in LCD panels and the like. When you refer to this displayed text, you can use an laternate font such as Courier. For example, "If the directory does not exist, the system will respond with No such file or directory." Or, "As the computer boots up, the digital read-out window will display 8888."

Extended code samples: In computer programming texts, extended programming samples are often shown in Courier.

— Screens and menus: This one may sound like the previous one on displayed text, but there is a difference. Menuing systems that do not use a graphical interface (which usually provides fancy proportional fonts) typical have a monospaced-font appearance. When a technical writer wants to show readers such menus, they use an alternate font like Courier. However, when they want to show screns or menus in a graphical interface (such as a Windows or Macintosh system), they use a screen capture in order to retain the authentic look of the screen.

Color: Color is used in technical text but it is expensive and hard to manage through the publishing cycle. However, color is easy to use in online information. It's common to see hypertext links, for example, using color. Online helps typically use green while web pages typically use blue for new links and purple for links the user has already explored.

The tendency to use color indiscriminately in online information is much like the tendency to go wild with bold, italics, type sizes, and alternate fonts in hardcopy information. The feeling must be something like, "It's there, it's cool, so let's use it!" There are not any strongly developed trends in the use of color in technical text, either online or hardcopy, other than the use of green and blue for hypertext links, mentioned earlier. Printed technical texts rarely use color because of the cost.

If you want to use color, plan it carefully. Don't expect readers to remember that red signals one idea, blue another idea, and green still some other idea. Just stick to one color. In general, avoid using color for extended text. Instead of making an entire warning notice red, just make the Warning label red and leave the warning text regular roman. Better still, read some of the standard literature on color in the technical communication field. There are general design issues and international issues:

Combinations of the preceding: In general, it's a bad idea to combine emphasis techniques, for example, bold and italics. In nonprofessional technical text, you'll see such garish combinations as all all-caps bold-italics or all-caps bold-italics with double quotation marks. Avoid these!. One legitimate combination is to use italics with alternate fonts.

Emphasis Techniques in Computer Text

Emphasis techniques used in computer texts vary widely. Here is a typical highlighting scheme for a user guide that discusses both hardware and software:

— Commands. Use bold for any command or subroutine, unless it is in an example. For example, "Use the move to change the name of the file."

— Variables, placeholders. Use italics for placeholder names for which readers substitute values. For example, "To change directories, use the cd NewDirectoryName command." Readers will replace NewDirectoryName with the name of an actual directory on their own computer.

— Text that the user enters. Use an alternate font, such as Courier, for text that readers must type in verbatim. For example, "To install the program, type setup speedpro and then press Enter." Courier is traditionally used because it resembles typewriter text, which resembles text on computer screens.

— Text displayed on the screen. Also use an alternate font, such as Courier, for text that is displayed on the computer, such as error messages. For example, "If the directory does not exist, the system will respond with No such file or directory." Or, "As the computer boots up, the digital read-out window will display 8888."

— Examples. Use an alternate font, such as Courier, for examples. The most common usage here is for extended code or representations of screens (such as menus).

— Menu and command buttons. Use bold for buttons on graphical user interfaces (Windows or Mac interfaces). For example, "Press Exit to exit the program." Or, "Press Format for a list of choices."

— Menu names. Use regular roman (the standard type style for body text, without emphasis) for meny or screen names, but copy the cap style used in the menu or screen. For example, "In the Format dialog box, you have a number of choices."

— Field names (labels). Use regular roman for field names (those text labels beside boxes in which you enter data or make choices), but copy the cap style used on the screen. For example, "In the Row to Delete Field, enter the number of rows you want to delete."

— Keyboard keys and mouse buttons. Use regular roman for names of keys on the keyboard, but copy the exact spelling and cap style. For example, "Press the Home key to move the text cursor to the beginning of the line." For mouse buttons, use lower case, for example, "Press the left mouse button."

— Extended emphasis. If any text more than two or three words must be emphasized, use special-notice format instead of making the extended text all bold, all italics, all caps, or some combination.

Although this highlighting scheme is fairly common, you may have spotted some areas of concern. For example, it might be confusing to readers for both example text and text they must enter to be Courier. They might mistake an example for text they must enter, or they might mistake required text for an example. It's considerations like these that explain the variability of highlighting schemes that you see in computer texts---along with the different needs of technology and readers.

13

Oral Technical Reports

For the oral report, imagine that you are formally handing over your final written report to the people with whom you set up the hypothetical contract or agreement. For example, imagine that you had contracted with a software company to write its user guide. Once you had completed it, you'd have a meeting with chief officers to formally deliver the guide. You'd spend some time orienting them to the guide, showing them how it is organized and written, and discussing some of its highlights. Your goal is to get them aquainted with the guide and to prompt them for any concerns or questions.

As you can see, you shouldn't have to do any research to prepare for this assignment—just plan the details of your talk and get at least one visual ready. If you have a topic that you'd prefer not to present orally to the group, discuss other possibilities with your instructor. Here are some brainstorming possibilities in case you want to present something else:

— *Purpose*: Another way to find a topic is to think about the purpose of your talk. Is it to instruct (for example, to explain how to run a text editing program on a computer), to persuade (to vote for or against a certain technically oriented bond issue), or simply to inform (to report on citizen participation in the new recycling program).

— *Informative purpose*: An oral report can be primarily informative. For example, as a member of a committee involved in a project to relocate the plant, your job might be to give an oral report on the condition of the building and grounds at one of the sites proposed for purchase. Or, you might be required to go before the city council and report on the success of the new city-sponsored recycling project.

— *Instructional purpose*: An oral report can be primarily instructional. Your task might be to train new employees to use certain equipment or to perform certain routine tasks.

— *Persuasive purpose*: An oral report can be primarily persuasive. You might want to convince members of local civic organizations to support a city-wide recycling program. You might appear before city council to persuade its members to reserve certain city-owned lands for park areas, softball and baseball parks, or community gardens.

— *Topics*: You can start by thinking of a technical subject, for example, solar panels, microprocessors, drip irrigation, or laser surgery. For your oral report, think of a subject you'd be interested in talking about, but find a reason why an audience would want to hear your oral report.

— *Place or situation*: You can find topics for oral reports or make more detailed plans for them by thinking about the place or the situation in which your oral report might naturally be given: at a neighborhood association? at the parent teachers' association meeting? at a church meeting? at the gardening club? at a city council meeting? at a meeting of the board of directors or high-level executives of a company? Thinking about an oral report this way makes you focus on the audience, their reasons for listening to you, and their interests and background.

The focus for your oral presentation is clear, understandable presentation; well-organized, well-planned, well-timed discussion. You don't need to be Mr. or Ms. Slick-Operator--just present the essentials of what you have to say in a calm, organized, well-planned manner. When you give your oral presentation, we'll all be listening for the same things. Use the following as a requirements list, as a way of focusing your preparations:

— Plan to explain to the class what the situation of your oral report is, who you are, and who they should imagine they are. Make sure that there is a clean break between this brief explanation and the beginning of your actual oral report.

— Make sure your oral report lasts no longer than 7 minutes. Your instructor will work out some signals to indicate when the 7-minute mark is approaching, has arrived, or has past.

— Pay special attention to the introduction to your talk. Indicate the purpose of your oral report, give an overview of its contents, and find some way to interest the audience.

— Use at least one visual--preferably a transparency for the overhead projector. Flip charts and objects for display are okay. But please avoid scribbling stuff on the chalkboard or relying strictly on handouts.

— Make sure you discuss key elements of your visuals. Don't just throw them up there and ignore them. Point out things about them; explain them to the audience.

— Make sure that your speaking style and gestures are okay. Ensure that you are loud enough so that everybody can hear, that you don't speak too rapidly (nerves often cause that), and that your gestures and posture are okay. For example, don't slouch on the podium or against the wall, and avoid fidgeting with your hands. As for speaking style, consider slowing your tempo a bit--a common tendency is to get nervous and talk too fast. Also, be aware of how much you say things like "uh," "you know," and "okay."

— Plan to explain any technical aspect of your topic very clearly and understandably. Don't race through complex, technical stuff--slow down and explain it carefully so that we understand it.

— Use "verbal headings"—by now, you've gotten used to using headings in your written work. There is a corollary in oral reports. With these, you give your audience a very clear signal you are moving from one topic or part of your talk to the next.

— Plan your report in advance and practice it so that it is organized. Make sure that listeners know what you are talking about and why, which part of the talk you are in, and what's coming next. Overviews and verbal headings greatly contribute to this sense of organization.

— End with a real conclusion. People sometimes forget to plan how to end an oral report and end by just trailing off into a mumble. Remember that in conclusions, you can summarize (go back over high points of what you've discussed), conclude (state some logical conclusion based on what you have presented), provide some last thought (end with some final interesting point but general enough not to require elaboration), or some combination of these three. And certainly, you'll want to prompt the audience for questions and concerns.

— As mentioned above, be sure your oral report is carefully timed to 7 minutes.

Oral Report Preparation

Pick the method of preparing for the talk that best suits your comfort level with public speaking and with your topic. However, do some sort of preparation or rehearsal—some people assume that they can just jump up there and ad lib for 7 minutes and be relaxed, informal. It doesn't often work that way—drawing a mental blank is the more common experience. Here are the obvious possibilities for preparation and delivery:

— Write a script, practice it, keep it around for quick-reference during your talk.

— Set up an outline of your talk, practice with it, bring it for reference.

— Set up cue cards, practice with them, use them during your talk.

— Write a script and read from it.

Of course, the extemporaneous or impromptu methods are also out there for the brave and the adventurous. However, please bear in mind that up to 25 people will be listening to you—you owe them a good presentation, one that is clear, understandable, well-planned, organized, and informative. It doesn't matter which method you use to prepare for the talk. Of course the head-down style of reading your report directly from a script has its problems. There is little or no eye contact or interaction with the audience.

The delivery tends toward a dull monotone that either puts listeners off or is hard to understand. For some reason, people tend to get nervous in this situation. Try to remember that your classmates and instructor are a very forgiving, supportive group. You don't have to be a slick entertainer--just be clear, organized, understandable, informative. The nerves will wear off someday, the more oral presenting you do.

When you give an oral report, focus on common problem areas such as these:

— *Timing*: Make sure you keep within the 7-minute time limit. Anything under 6 minutes is also a problem. Do some rehearsal, write a script, or find some other way to get the timing just right.

— *Volume*: Obviously, you must be sure to speak loud enough so that all of your audience can hear you. You might find some way to practice speaking a little louder in the days before the oral presentation.

— *Pacing, speed*: Sometimes, oral presentators who are a bit nervous talk too fast. All that adrenaline causes them to speed through their talk. That makes it hard for the audience to follow. In general, it helps listeners to understand you better if you speak a bit more slowly and deliberately than you do in normal conversation. Slow down, take it easy, be clear.

— *Gestures and posture*: Watch out for nervous hands flying all over the place. This too can be distracting--and a bit comical. At the same time, don't turn yourself into a mannikin. Plan to keep your hands clasped together or holding onto the podium and only occasionally making some gesture. As for posture, avoid slouching at the podium and leaning against the wall.

— *Verbal crutches*: Watch out for too much "uh," "you know," "okay" and other kinds of nervous verbal habits. Instead of saying "uh" or "you know" every three seconds, just don't say anything at all. In the days before your oral presentation, practice speaking without these verbal crutches. The silence that replaces them is not a bad thing--it gives listeners time to process what you are saying.

Here are some ideas for the "medium" to use for your visuals:

— *Transparencies for overhead projector*: For most college classrooms and, in fact, business conference rooms, the overhead projector is the best way to show things to the whole group. Design your visual on a sheet of blank paper, then photocopy it, and then get a transparency of it. You may have access to equipment like this at your work; most copy shops can make transparencies for you; and your instructor can make transparencies for you, given a few days lead-time.

— *Posterboard-size charts*: Another possibility is to get some posterboard and draw and letter what you want your audience to see. If you have a choice, consider transparencies--it's hard to make charts look neat and professional.

— *Handouts*: You can run off copies of what you want your listeners to see and hand them out before or during your talk. This option is even less effective than the first two because you can't point to what you want your listeners to see and because handouts take listeners' attention away from you. Still, for certain visual needs, handouts are the only choice.

— *Objects*: If you need to demonstrate certain procedures, you may need to bring in actual physical objects. Rehearse what you are going to do with these objects; sometimes they can take up a lot more time than you expect.

Please avoid just scribbling your visual on the chalkboard. Whatever you can scribble on the chalkboard can be neatly prepared and made into a transparency or posterboard-size chart, for example. Take some time to make your visuals look sharp and professional-use a straightedge, good dark markers, neat lettering or typing. Do your best to ensure that they are legible to the entire audience. As for the content of your visuals consider these ideas:

— *Drawing or diagram of key objects*: If you describe or refer to any objects during your talk, try to get visuals of them so that you can point to different components or features.

— *Tables, charts, graphs*: If you discuss statistical data, present it in some form or table, chart, or graph. Many members of your audience may have trouble "hearing" such data as opposed to seeing it.

— *Outline of your talk, report, or both*: If you are at a loss for visuals to use in your oral presentation, or if your presentation is complex, have an outline of it that you can show at various points during your talk.

— *Key terms and definitions*: A good idea for visuals (especially when you can't think of any others) is to set up a two-column list of key terms you use during your oral presentation with their definitions in the second column.

— *Key concepts or points*: Similarly, you can list your key points and show them in visuals. (Outlines, key terms, and main points are all good, legitimate ways of incorporating visuals into oral presentations when you can't think of any others.)

During your actual oral report, make sure to discuss your visuals, refer to them, guide your listeners through the key points in your visuals. It's a big problem just to throw a visual up on the screen and never even refer to it.

Effective Presentations

An essential aspect of any research project is dissemination of the findings arising from the study. The most common ways to make others aware of your work is by publishing the results in a journal article, or by giving an oral or poster presentation (often at a regional or national meeting). While efforts are made to teach the elements of writing a journal article in many graduate school curricula, much less attention is paid to teaching those skills necessary to develop a good oral or poster presentation - even though these arguably are the most common and most rapid ways to disseminate new findings. In addition, the skills needed to prepare an oral presentation can be used in a variety of other settings - such as preparing a seminar in graduate school, organizing a dissertaton defense, conducting a job interview seminar, or even addressing potential philanthropic sources!

Effective oral communication is an important - but often overlooked and underpracticed - skill in scientific and academic endeavors. This tutorial has been developed to serve as an introductory guide and general reference for use when formulating a talk. The principles should be applied whenever you are faced with making a public presentation, whether it's a journal club presentation or a more formal talk, such as a conference presentations, job talks, and invited seminars.

There are very few people having a natural talent for delivering outstanding presentations (IMHO, anyway). On the other hand, foresight, hard work, and practice can carry most of the rest of us into the 'very good' level of presentation skills. The standards for public speaking in the scientific and academic realms are relatively low, so a good presentation often is memorable.

Initial Planning

This is where you begin to tailor the talk to the situation, and for that reason this stage is very important for a successful presentation. Talk to your host and clarify these points before you spend much preparation time. If the environment and audience are unfamiliar to you, this is a critical stage. You may even want to do a literature search on potential audience members to identify areas of common interest or potential questions which may arise. Begin this stage early - the more lead time you allow yourself, the more time you will have to think up novel approaches to the topic and the more interesting and substantial your presentation will be. Before you begin preparing the presentation, you'll need to determine:

1. The type of talk you will be expected to give
   - — will this be an informal chat, a seminar discussion, or a more formal presentation?
   - — different talks have different purposes; the intent of a conference presentation is not the same as a job talk. When in doubt, ask for guidance from your host.
2. The composition of the audience
   - — will you be speaking to a general audience or specialists?
   - — how many people are expected to attend?
   - — is this likely to be a friendly audience? An interactive audience?
3. The time allotted for the talk
   - — the longer the talk, the more freedom you will have to explore the topic
   - — a short talk needs to be very clear and to address the topic directly
   - — is question time included?
4. Expectations for information content

— is there a specific purpose for having you give a talk? Clarify the expectations beforehand and plan to address them during the presentation.

— will you be presenting novel concepts to this audience, or building upon their prior knowledge? Either way, make sure you cover the basics clearly, and early in the talk, to avoid loosing the audience.

Once you have a general idea of what you want to say, you'll have to decide how to say it. Unlike a conversation or a written document, a talk is a one-shot attempt to make a point. By contrast, a conversation consists of repetitions and clarification's based on questions and immediate feedback, while a written paper allows a reader to puzzle through its contents as often as necessary. It is essential that your talk be well-constructed and tidy, and that your points be presented to the audience both a logical sequence and unambiguously. This all takes a fair amount of preparation. Start early! Here are a few pointers to get you started:

1. Start preparing far in advance by thinking through what needs to be said. Collect material which may relate to the topic from unusual sources, and sleep on these ideas. The final product will be more fully-developed and interesting.

2. Using big letters and a bold pen, write a clear statement of the problem and its importance, and then pin that statement on the wall above your desk.

3. Develop this theme into one jargon-free sentence that will catch the attention of the audience. Next, identify the issues you plan to address (brainstorm, then trim back; see the portion of this tutorial on outlining).

4. Arrange these issues in a logical sequence (which may change as you develop the talk). This process is easier if you use index cards to organize your talk, with one idea per card.

5. Computer-based presentation programs (PowerPoint, Persuasion, etc.) can be wonderful time-savers. The time invested in learning to use these programs is rewarded by the speed with which a presentation can be created, even by a moderately-skilled user. These programs are good tools for organizing your presentation (an electronic version of the index cards idea), they can be used to create visuals for the presentation (e.g., slides and transparencies), and even project those visuals during the presentation.

6. Avoid using lists (First..., Second...); you may confuse listing systems (First..., Point B..., and another thing...), or you may discover later in the talk that you've missed

a point entirely, and then you'll be forced to backtrack. Both of these problems tend to distract your audience away from the points you are trying to make, and both give the appearance of poor organizational skills.

7. Retention of information by the audience is reduced as a talk proceeds, so if you do want to make a series of points, organize them from the most to the least important. That way, the audience is more likely to remember the important points later. You may even find that the less important points become irrelevant to the focus of the talk as you practice.

8. Determine transition elements which will help your audience to follow the link from one issue to the next. These should be logical, and may presented by posing a question, or explaining your own discovery of the link's existence.

9. Use short sentences with simple constructions. The concept will be made more clear, and the sentence structure is more similar to conversational styles.

10. Run through the talk once, early. Go back and re-think the sequencing. Discard non-essential elements.

11. Don't assume the audience will be familiar with basic concepts that form the foundation of your talk. Outline these concepts briefly but clearly early in the talk to avoid confusion.

12. Attempt to identify problems or questions the audience may have and address them in the talk, before the audience has a chance to think of these things themselves.

13. Determine which elements would benefit by being presented with visual aids. Spend time working out the best way to present the material. Head on over to the accompanying tutorials for information on presenting material in an effective way using visual aids.

14. Prepare thumbnails sketches of these visual aids, then run through the talk again. Re-work the most appropriate and essential visual aids and discard the rest. Don't forget to proof-read your visuals! Do so while there is plenty of time to re-print that critical slide with the glaring typo.

15. The earlier you start on the visuals, the better they will be. On the other hand, avoid fine tuning each visual endlessly; if you find yourself diddling the details, go on to do something more productive instead.

16. When in doubt about which presentation medium to use (transparencies, slides, videos, multimedia, etc.), choose the format which is the least complex which remains consistent with both clarity and content of the presentation. Keep in mind that the more technology you use, the more things there will be which can go wrong. These technological difficulties may develop into a gruesome presentation experience, particularly if you are giving the talk in an unfamiliar setting!

17. If you do need to use multimedia technology in your presentation, call ahead to make sure the technology you require is supported in the room where you'll be talking!

18. The most important preparation factor is to REHEARSE! Do so in private at first. Then for a real acid test, videotape yourself and watch the results with a critical eye. It's often a painful and humbling experience, but the results will be worth it.

19. You can then try the presentation out in front of a few colleagues. Ask for feedback, then act on that information. Select those who know a little about your topic, and not those who know a lot. This will focus your attention on attempting to explain why you did what you did in simple terms, rather than encouraging attention to details only specialists care about.

20. If you start preparing early, you'll have plenty of time to refine the presentation based on your colleagues' feedback. This is always a useful process.

21. Don't waste your colleagues' time; if you are sincere about wanting that feedback, don't wait until the night before the presentation to ask for other people's input.

22. Remember, the shorter the talk, the more difficult it will be to cover the material clearly and completely. Be strict about including only what is essential information for the presentation, and removing all the non-essential tidbits.

The primary purpose of a presentation is to provide information which the audience will then remember at a later date. Detailed referencing of material or extensive review of data won't be remembered - and may put the audience to sleep!

One way to maintain interest is to organize and present the material in a novel manner. Using a non-standard ordering of material will help to keep the audience interested. Similarly, organizing your material in a new way (rather than re-working an old talk) will help to keep your own interest in the topic, and will result in a talk which is more fresh and exciting. The importance of outlining is often stressed in preparing written and oral presentations, but an outline following a linear format (headings, subheadings, etc.) may be restrictive.

A list of terms and ideas can be daunting, and tends to focus attention on the final items. Consider creating an 'idea network' as an alternative approach for organizing your presentation (or your written paper). A question that often is asked at this stage is "Is this enough material for the talk?". Actually, you'll probably find that you have far too much material. It is important to develop a realistic view of how much material is appropriate, and the ability to be ruthless in eliminating non-essential material. These abilities vary widely among presenters, and are important factors in determining the quality of the presentation. Here are a few guidelines for helping determine how much material is enough...

Pre-determining the content in relation to length is always a problem. The magnitude of the task will become more obvious as you begin to practice. Remember that when you make allowances for a new setting and being interrupted by questions, the practice talk will be about 20% faster than the real presentation. Two ways people try to reduce the length of a presentation are to speak more quickly and to reduce the number of words used. Both produce a false economy - the practice talk will fit in your time frame, but the final product won't.

In fact, one good strategy is to be very selective about what you need to say, then say only that - and say it clearly with slightly longer pauses between words than normal. Increasing the length of inter-word pauses will force you to enunciate the ending of one word and the beginning of the next word - making it easier for the audience to follow what you are saying. This is a particularly good strategy for people giving a presentation a language that is not their native language. Fewer words, spoken clearly....

Try the following suggestions to get into a good ballpark range:

— Estimate a rate of about 100 words per minute (slow! - conversation occurs at about 300 words/minute)

— Each statement you make will require an average of 12 words

— Each concept will need to be supported by 3 - 4 statements

That means for a 50 minute talk, you should expect to cover only about 90 concepts. One way to facilitate the process is to develop visual aids which illustrate your points clearly. Check out the accompanying tutorials for more details about preparing visual aids. Once again, if you possess idiosyncratic pronunciations (e.g., an accent) then place the troublesome word in the slide's text and point to that word as you say it - make it easy for the audience to figure out what you mean to say!

Keeping these elements in mind as you prepare and practice the presentation will reduce the amount of reworking you'll have to do as it evolves, and will result in a more streamlined and effective end product.

1. *Rate*: The optimal rate for a scientific talk is about 100 words per minute. Any faster and the audience can't absorb the additional information. Use pauses, and repeat critical information.

2. *Opening*: The opening should catch the interest and attention of the audience immediately, while avoiding trite filler phrases and technical jargon.

3. *Transitions*: The link between successive elements of the talk should be planned carefully, smooth, and logical. You should make the relation between successive elements clear to the audience.

4. *Conclusion*: Summarize the main concepts you've discussed, and how your work relates to issues you've raised. Aim to help your audience achieve high retention of this final information. Signal that the summary is beginning ("In summary,..."), but don't begin the summary too soon or else the audience will start to leave before you finish!

5. *Length*: Don't run over! Ever! Shorten your talk by removing details, concepts, and information, not by eliminating words. If it becomes absolutely essential to supply details, supplement your presentation with a handout. Make about 10% more handouts than you think you'll need. Always leave time for a few questions at the end of the talk.

Remember that there is no point in giving a presentation if the audience isn't listening. You should make a big effort to help them be interested in what you have to say. It therefore is appropriate to use techniques to retain audience interest, provided these techniques don't detract from the content or professionalism of the talk.

Practice is the single most important factor contributing to a good presentation. No matter how rushed you might be, make time for at least a few practice runs. The effects of practice will be apparent, and a poorly presented talk reflects upon both you and your attitude towards the material and audience. Don't be fooled by people who claim to be able to throw together a talk at a moment's notice.

Generally, their talks fall into two categories - talks which are disjointed and awkward, and talks which have had the rough edges removed by numerous prior presentations (i.e., dull and unexciting). One problem is that you can waste a tremendous amount of time by practicing all the wrong parts of your talk. It is necessary to run through the talk a few times to get an idea of how the talk will flow. After that, seek some outside feedback to make sure you are on the right track. Finally, practice all parts of the talk equally. If you always start at the beginning and work until you run into problems, the beginning of the talk will be great, but the final portion of the talk will be relatively more weak.

Begin one out of every few practice runs in the middle or at the end of the talk. Yes, that means running through the talk once or twice isn't enough, particularly if the material is new to you. If the presentation is important, treat it that way. Practice. Having spent all that time preparing the talk itself, there are still a few things you can do at the last minute which will help ensure a successful presentation. Or, if you are the nervous type, help fill time...

1. Before the day begins, or last thing the night before, run through your talk once more. Use a mirror or visualize standing in front of an audience as you practice. If you've brought a slide carousel with you (a good idea), check their arrangement. You probably won't have time to do this later. Remember to seat the locking ring properly!

2. If possible, take a tour the room you'll use for the presentation early in the day. Look for potential problems with line of sight due to furniture, dark spots due to dead overhead lights, intruding sound from ventilation - these all can be fixed with a bit of prior warning and a polite request.

3. If you need specialized equipment, make sure it is available ahead of time - don't spring that information on your host at the last minute.

4. Check again to see that your slides are oriented properly in the carousel. Lock that ring!

5. Make sure the focus switch works, and determine who will be controlling the slide advance. Do the slide advance, reverse, and focus features all work?

6. It's your show, so ask for help with the equipment if you need it; it's better to ask for help then fumble around during the presentation. Determine who will be controlling equipment for you.

7. Computer presentations introduce a whole host of potential issues - here are a few to consider:

   — Is the host software compatible with your presentation? Are the fonts, bullets, colors, etc. the same?

   — Is there a sound card in the host computer? Is the sound system operational - but not too painfully loud?

   — Back-up your presentation before you leave using an alternate medium, then bring it with you separately from the one you plan to use (e.g., packed in a different suitcase), or e-mail it to yourself as an attachment - you may be able to access it from your destination if needed.

— Alternatively, e-mail it to your host and ask that her or she download the file and test it on the computer you'll be using - Before you depart for the trip!

— Did you include all the required files and resources for your presentation?

— You might consider making a set of 35mm presentation slides from your electronic presentation, then bringing the stack of slides along as your fail-safe backup - this strategy may depend upon your degree of compulsiveness and/or paranoia, or how important the presentation is to you.

— Keep in mind that failures of technology can be devestating, but that 1) the embrassment is greater on the part of the host if their equipment is at fault, and 2) the host is usually impressed if you provide an alternate solution to the problem - suggesting you are a proactive and prepared person....

8. Irrespective of what your presentation medium might be, letting your presentation slides, disk, CD, etc. out of your sight before the presentation begins can lead to disaster.

9. If the room is large, or your voice small, use a microphone. Try it out before the audience arrives (blowing into the mike or counting '1-2-3' they have arrived is tacky, so don't do it).

10. Check to see that accessories are present; chalk, eraser, markers, and especially a pointer. If it is a laser pointer, does it have fresh batteries loaded? Keep in mind that green wavelength lasers DEVOUR batteries!

11. Avoid standing behind a lectern or desk during the presentation. Stand to one side of the projection screen or blackboard, and closer to the audience if possible.

12. Moderate movement and hand gestures are OK, but avoid pacing and flapping.

13. Don't be afraid to insist on a few minutes to yourself prior to the talk; 15 to 30 minutes is standard. If you have an itinerary, check to see that you've had time allotted for preparation. If you are running behind, see if someone is willing to meet with you after the talk, then use that time to prepare instead. Use this time to double-check your materials, and your introductory and summary statements. Don't allow yourself to be distracted by audience members coming up to chat.

14. Don't wait until the very last minute to make that run to the bathroom, and remember to check carefully your appearance - including zippers, buttons and other closures - before you reappear.

Moment of Truth

Gulp. So you are sitting there, about to be introduced. Now what?

1. Take several deep breaths as you are being introduced (but don't sigh!). Visualize your rehearsed opening statement; don't improvise at the last moment.

2. State your objectives at start of your talk, then restate them again at the end of the talk. In between, discuss how your material relates to these objectives.

3. Unless you intentionally have had experience as a stand-up comic, avoid making jokes. The results can be disappointing, and may suggest an unprofessional attitude.

4. Choose a natural, moderate rate of speech and use automatic, moderate gestures.

5. Monitor your behavior, and avoid habitual behaviors (pacing, fumbling change in pocket, twirling hair).

6. Laser pointers are wonderful pointing devices, but remember not to point them at the audience. They are best used by flashing the pointer on and off, so that the place you are indicating is illuminated briefly. Don't swirl the laser around and around one place on the projection screen, or sweep it from place to place across the screen. This is very distracting for the audience, and they will end up watching the pointer and not listening to what you are saying.
7. Likewise, and for the same reasons, avoid using the cursor as in pointer in your computer presentations.
8. Also try to avoid pointing things out on the computer's monitor at the podium - although the presenter's natural tendency is to concentrate on the monitor's screen, the audience will be looking over your shoulder at the projection screen and won't be able to see where your finger is pointing. If you find yourself doing this, power-off or disable the monitor to force yourself to concentrate on the projection screen!
9. Enthusiasm for your topic is contagious, but don't overdo it - you'll alienate the audience.
10. Converse with your audience. Involve them in the process of the presentation by posing questions and making eye contact. Be patient if you ask a question - answers sometimes take time to formulate.
11. Keep an eye on your time, and don't run over your limit. Ever.
12. Be prepared for interruptions (late arrivals, cell phones or pagers, burned out projector bulbs, fire drills, etc.).
13. If you must turn down the room lights, don't turn them off entirely. Don't leave the lights down any longer than necessary - remember to turn them back up! Of course, the snores from the sleeping audience may remind you to turn the lights back on if you've forgotten.

14. Don't apologize for any aspect of your presentation. This should be your very best effort; if you have to apologize, you haven't done your job properly.

15. Don't criticize aspects of the trip, city, facilities, etc. during your talk. This is another way to alienate your audience quickly. For instance, they may or may not have chosen to live in this horrible climate, but it isn't your place to remind them how horrible it is. Remember that you are a guest and it is impolite to exhibit your prejudices publically.

16. Strive to have a prepared and memorable summary. If nothing else, the take home message is what the audience will remember after you leave.

17. When you reach the summary and are about to finish, resist the temptation to add a few last impromptu words. They will be unpracticed, and will be the last thing many of your audience will hear you say. End your talk with the insightful, firm summary statement you have prepared.

18. Don't be afraid to give yourself credit for your own work, but do remember to give others credit where due. If planned for later in the talk, don't forget to acknowledge these people's efforts, even if you have to skip a statement or two to remain within your time frame. The best friend of one of these contibutors may be in your audience! If you include slides borrowed from other people, or slides which include other people's data or figures, always give credit to these people right on that slide. This shows a professional attitude, and (better yet) can save you many words of explanation.

Management of Questions

Your presentation doesn't end once you've finished what you have to say. The question period often is the part of the talk which influences the audience the most. After all, you've had time to practice the rest of the talk. This is the part of the presentation where your ability to interact with the audience will be evaluated. Since you can't always predict the what you'll be asked, how can you prepare for the questioning? Here are a few guidelines:

1. Always repeat each question so the entire audience knows what you've been asked.

2. Before you answer, take a moment to reflect on the question. By not rushing to give an answer, you show a degree of respect for the questioner, and you give yourself time to be sure you are answering the question that actually was asked. If you are unsure, restate the question or ask for a clarification.

3. Above all, wait for the questioner to finish asking the question before you begin your answer! The only exception is when it becomes necessary to break in on a vague, rambling question; this is your show, and you have only a limited time to make your presentation. It is essential, however, that you break in tactfully. Say something like "So, are you asking....?" This will focus the question and give you a place to begin an answer. Remember that your ability to interact with an audience also is being evaluated.

4. If a question is asked during the talk, and it will clarify an ambiguity, answer it immediately.

5. Postpone questions aimed at resolving specific problems (or arcane knowledge) until the end of the talk, or private discussion. This is particularly important if the answer will distract either you or the audience away from the flow of your presentation.

6. Avoid prolonged discussions with one person, extended answers, and especially arguments.

7. If you can't answer a question, just say so. Don't apologize. You then may:

— Offer to research an answer, then get back to the questioner later.

— Suggest resources which would help the questioner to address the question themselves.

— Ask for suggestions from the audience.

The following information may be presented elsewhere in these tutorials, but are worth considering again here!

Question and Answer Slide

The question & answer slide is the slide that follows your conclusions and remains in the background as you answer questions from the audience. A very good idea is to carefully select the most important images from your prior slides, shrink them so they all fit on this slide, then arrange them so that they are up for the audience to see as they Q & A session goes on. This will allow them to consider your data and interpretations without having to recall details, it gives them a chance to reconsider the information after you've delivered the 'big question' answer, and it helps you to guide the content of the Q&A session to meet your own ends.

Avoid:

— turning off the projector (you'll just have to turn it on again - and wait while it warms up).

— projecting a blank white (dazzling) or blank black (too dark) slide

— leaving your conclusion slide in place as you answer questions.

Acknowledgements Slide

This is an important slide! No one works in a vacumn, nor are many scientists sufficiently wealthy to fund their own research without outside sources! On the other hand, avoid reading a list of names and agencies as this:

— takes time

— typically is information of little interest to the audience

— may give the appearance of 'name dropping'

— no one will remember names of people they don't know anyway

But this is important - particularly if a collaborator's best friend is sitting in the audience! Consider using a collage of photos of your collaborators in their natural settings for this purpose. You may still point out the primary collaborators, but a visual approach is inherently more interesting for the audience. Moreover, at a crowded conference a collaborator is more likely to be recognized in the hallway or at a restaurant if your audience has seen his or her photo during your talk. You should consider carefully the content of the photo, however, if you are presenting it in a professional setting!

While most people can, however unwillingly, stand in front of an audience and talk, an exciting and effective presentation requires organization and thought ahead of time. Keep in mind that a first year undergraduate has logged around 13,000 classroom hours; add about another 1,200 hours by the time they reach graduate school and get feisty about sitting through dull lectures. These are, you might say, "educated" consumers of the classroom experience.

But for a really tough group, imagine an audience of jaded academics and researchers attending a scientific conference! A focused and understandable communication of ideas underlies all forms of academic and scholarly communication, whether in the form of a written paper, a presentation at a scientific meeting, leading a seminar discussion, or presenting a lecture to students. Your decisions about which visual aids to use and how to maximize their visual impact can make a striking difference in the strength and clarity of your presentation.

Here are Some Guidelines that will help you to pull off a good presentation, by helping to increase the impact of the visuals you will use.

To Begin with...

The first step is to outline your presentation, identify the major concepts and principle points you plan to make, then determine which will of these require a visual for clarity. Next, make a sketch of each visual. Title slides are a great idea, but don't go overboard on the artwork. Ask yourself which you would rather have the audience remember - the artwork or the content. Be sure that the title will be interpreted by the audience the way you intend it to be, and check for spelling errors!

One of the early visuals often is used to break the ice, warming the audience up and getting you over the jitters (but if that's not your style, don't bother - nothing is more awkward that watching someone tell a joke when they don't posess that talent). Using an icebreaker is fine, but don't overuse cartoons. You'll want to avoid appearing shallow or superficial. Screen the contents and implications of each cartoon carefully, too.

Another common use of a visual is to introduce or acknowledge collaborators. Consider placing this near the front end of the talk. That way it will only take a few seconds early on when you feel there is plenty of time - and it won't get lost at the end of the talk when you may feel temporally constrained. Collaborators can be listed by name and affiliation, but a more effective way to acknowledge these folks is a collage of candid photos with names attached. If one or more of the collaborators is in the audience, this can be great fun, and can serve as an icebreaker.

If you pay attention to these four concepts as you put the visuals together, the end products will be effective.

1) Make it BIG
2) Keep it Simple
3) Make it Clear
4) Be Consistent

If you plan to export your efforts as a data file, and eventually to use imaging software to create a series of presentation slides, consider this. Most rolls of film come as 24 or 36 exposures, and the difference in purchase & developing costs is negligible. Consider buying 36 exposure rolls, and filling the leftover exposures with copies of your key visuals. This means you'll have extra copies for those times when you'd have to forward & reverse through a series of slides in order to make a particular point. You'll also have copies for when you misplace that critical slide...

Here are the final words in this tutorial.

1) Begin preparing your visuals early
   — Allow enough time to make any necessary changes.
   — Project the visuals to verify content, spelling, sizes, and colors
   — Practice the presentation with the visuals.
   — Take the time to reconsider the presentation as a whole.
2) Make back-up copies frequently
3) Practice the presentation. A lot.

Poster Presentation

A poster presentation should guide each viewer through the basics of the study, freeing the presenter to focus on discussion of essential elements of the work. Decisions about poster format and design contribute to efficient and accurate transfer of information using this medium.

Read the Instructions supplied by the meeting organizers! Having an idea about these details before you begin will make the whole process much easier.

General format

1. Determine the one essential concept you would like to get across to the audience.

2. Re-read your abstract once again - are those statements still accurate?

3. Determine the size of the poster (if you had read the instructions, you would already know this!).

4. Determine if you have all the elements you'll need for the poster: Bits & pieces? Poster board, glue, razor blades, Bandaids... Data? Do you have the data you will need? How much time will you need to prepare the data for presentation (tables, photographs, etc.)? Outside agencies? Does material need to be sent out & returned (photographic services, collaborators)?

—A word of advice (the first of many; pick and choose what works for you). Preparing a poster will take as much time as you let it. Allocate your time wisely.

— There are always things that go wrong, so do not wait until the last minute to do even a simple task.

— This is a public presentation; by planning carefully, striving to be clear in what you say and how you say it, and assuming a professional attitude you will avoid making it a public spectacle.

— If you have little experience making posters, it will take longer (estimate 1 week at the very minimum).

— Too much lead time, however, encourages endless fussing about. Do the poster to the best of your ability, then go do something else.

Title Banner

This part of the poster includes the title of the work, the authors names, the institutional affiliations, and the poster number. Think BIG!

1. The title banner should be readable from 15 - 20 feet away.
2. If space permits, use first names for authors to facilitate interactions.
3. Middle initials and titles are seldom necessary, however.
4. Use abbreviations where possible.
5. City names, or even states, often may be dropped from the institutional affiliations.
6. There are seldom rules regarding line justification of the title. Determine if you will left or center justify the text of the title banner once it has been formatted, based upon personal preferences and space constraints.
7. Refer to your meeting guidelines for more details specific to the meeting you plan to attend.

Mount poster materials on colored art, mat, or bristol board:

1. Mat board is available in a large range of colors.
2. Mat board is heavier, making it more difficult to crease the poster while traveling.
3. Mat board has a more durable surface than other art papers.
4. Mat boards is, however, heavier and more difficult to attach to display boards in the poster session.

Use a colored background to unify your poster:

1. Muted colors, or shades of gray, are best for the background. Use more intense colors as borders or for emphasis, but be conservative - overuse of color is distracting.

2. Two to three related background colors (Methods, Data, Interpretation) will unify the poster.
3. If necessary for emphasis, add a single additional color by mounting the figure on thinner poster board, or outlining the figure in colored tape.

Color can enhance the hues or contrast of photographs:

1. Use a light background with darker photos; a dark background with lighter photos.
2. Use a neutral background (gray) to emphasize color in photos; a white background to reduce the impact of colored photos.
3. Most poster sessions are held in halls lit with harsh fluorescent light. If exact colors are important to the data, balance those colors for use with fluorescent lighting. Also, all colors will be intensified; bright (saturated) colors may become unpleasent to view.

Illustrations

— The success of a poster directly relates to the clarity of the illustrations and tables.

— Self-explanatory graphics should dominate the poster.

— A minimal amount of text materials should supplement the graphic materials.

— Use regions of empty space between poster elements to differentiate and accentuate these elements.

— Graphic materials should be visible easily from a minimum distance of 6 feet.

— Restrained use of 2 - 3 colors for emphasis is valuable; overuse is not.

Poster Text

— Double-space all text, using left-justification; text with even left sides and jagged right sides is easiest to read.

— The text should be large enough to be read easily from at least 6 feet away.

— Section headings (Introduction, Methods, etc.); use Helvetica, Boldface, 36 point

— Supporting text (Intro text, figure captions, etc.); use Helvetica, 24 point (boldface, if appropriate)

— If you must include narrative details, keep them brief. They should be no smaller than 18 point in size, and printed in plain text. Remember that posters are not publications of record, and you can always come to the session armed with handouts.

One option is to consider using a larger size (36 pt) for the Conclusion text, and a smaller size (18 pt) for Methods text. Attempt to fit blocks of text onto a single page:

— This simplifies cutting and pasting when you assemle the poster.

— For the same reason, consider using 11 x 14 inch paper in the landscape mode when printing text blocks on laser printers.

Other options for fonts include Helvetica, Arial, Geneva, Times Roman, Palatino, Century Schoolbook, Courier, and Prestige. Note that these fonts represent a range of letter spacing and letter heights. Keep in mind that san serif fonts (having characters without curliques or other embellishments) are easiest to read. Finally, be consistent. Choose one font and then use it throughout the poster. Add emphasis by using boldface, underlining, or color; italics are difficult to read.

Background of aPoster

Two basic rules to keep in mind are that

1) Artistry does not substitute for content

2) The fancier the poster, the greater the time investment.

There are several common approaches. Some folks use pieces of mat board (or Bristol board) to make a solid background for the entire poster. They may then choose to use a complementary color as a border for important elements of the poster. Others use smaller pieces of board to frame only the elements of the poster, leaving spaces between the elements empty.

Either approach works; the former gives a unified appearence and is easier to hang straight, while the latter is easier to carry to and from the meeting. It is also possible, but often expensive, to have a commercial house reproduce your completed poster as a single large sheet of paper, which can then be rolled into a cylinder for transport. The choice of a background (and complement) color is up to you. The general consensus, however, is that softer colors (pastels, greys) work best as a background - they are easiest to view for hours at a time, and offer the best contrast for text, graphic, and photographic elements.

14

Designing Electronic Documents

Electronic Document

Every text that is not delivered as an electronic document on a floppy disc, a magnetic tape, or via a computer network will have to be put into the system manually. Re-typing a text into the computer solely to make it available for MT is unlikely to be cost-effective — it would often be quicker to have the text translated directly by a human translator. In recent years it has become practicable to use an optical character reader (OCR) to input text available only in printed form. Clearly this is much quicker than re-typing, but checking for and correcting scanning errors can be time-consuming.

However, if as is the case with ETRANS, the MT system fits into an overall document production system (DPS), then text can be created, translated, re-edited and generally prepared for publication within the same electronic environment. Electronic text is simply text which is available in a machine readable form. For example, electronic text is produced by ordinary office word processors. At its simplest, such a text is just a sequence of characters, and, for the characters in use in general computing (i.e. the English alphabet, normal punctuation characters, plus characters such as the 'space' character, the 'line-feed' character, etc.) there is a standard representation provided by the ASCIIcodes, which associates each character with a seven or eight bit code.

Unfortunately, this standard is not sufficient for encoding the letters of foreign alphabets and their accents, even those based on the Roman alphabet, let alone non-Roman alphabets, and characters in non-alphabetic scripts, such as Japanese characters (Kanji). One approach to such alphabets is to extend the ASCII codes beyond those needed by English. Another is to represent foreign accents and special characters by sequences of standard ASCII characters. For example, a German *u* with umlaut (*ü*) might be represented thus: \"{u}. One problem is that there is (as yet) no genuine accepted standard beyond basic ASCII, with the further complication that many word processors use non-ASCII representations 'internally', as a way of representing text format (e.g. information about typeface, underlining, etc.) This lack of standards means that it is necessary to use special conversion programs if one wants to freely import and export text from different languages and a variety of DPSs (such as word processors).

Even when such programs exist, they do not always preserve all the information (e.g. some information about format may be lost). Part of a general solution to these problems, however, is to distinguish two components of a printed document: the text itself (a sequence of words and characters); and its rendition — the form in which it appears on the page (or screen). For example, consider a title or heading. There are the words which make up the title — perhaps a noun phrase such as 'The Electronic Document' — and the particular presentation or rendition of those words on the page.

If we think about this distinction between text and rendition in electronic terms, it is easy to see that we have to code both the characters in the text, and indicate how we intend parts of that text to appear on screen or in printed form. In the early days of electronic text handling, this problem was solved in a rather direct and obvious fashion: the author would type in not only the substance of the text but also some special codes at appropriate places to tell the printer to switch into the appropriate type faces and point size. For example, in typing in a title the author would carefully insert an appropriate number of carriage returns (non-printing characters which start a newline) to get a nice spacing before and after. She would also make sure the title was centred or left-aligned as required, and finally she would type in special codes (say \[223\[-447) before and after the title string to switch the printer into a bold typeface with 24 'points' to the inch and back to its usual font and size immediately afterwards.

There are three evident problems with such a procedure:

1 The codes used are likely to be specific to particular printers or word processing setups and hence the electronic document will not be directly portable to other systems for revision, integration with other documents or printing.

2 The author is required to spend some of her time dealing with rendition problems-a task that (prior to the advent of electronic systems) had always been conveniently delegated to the compositor in a printing house.

3 If at some point it is decided that a different rendition of headings is required, someone has to go through the entire document and replace all the codes and characters associated with the rendition of each heading.

The printer codes are a sort of tiny little program for a particular printer. The next development was to replace these rather specific programs by some means of stating directly "I want this in 24 point Roman boldface" — perhaps by a 'markup' like this: '`\roman\24pt\bf` '. Each printer or word processor can then be equipped with a special program (a so-called 'driver') which interprets this high-level code and sends the printer or screen appropriate specific low-level codes. Providing everyone used exactly the same high-level codes in all systems, the problem of portability would be solved. However, there is another way of tackling the rendition problem.

When one thinks about it abstractly, the only thing that the author really needs to put into the text is some markup which says (in effect) 'This is a heading', or 'This is a footnote' or 'This is an item in an item list' and so on. Each piece of text is thus identified as being an instance of some class of text elements. With such markup, the author no longer has to worry about how each such marked document element is going to be printed or shown on screen — that task can be delegated to the document designer (the modern equivalent of a compositor).

The document designer can specify an association between each type of document element and the high-level rendition codes she wants it to have. In other words, she can say that she wants all headings to be printed in 24 point boldface Romn. The document handling system then ensures that headings etc. are displayed and printed as required. This type of markup, where the author simply identifies particular pieces of text as being instances of particular document elements, is known as descriptive or 'intensional' ('intentional') markup. This notion is fundamental to all modern document processing systems and techniques.

Not only does this provide flexibility in how text is rendered, provided that the way in which markup is made is consistent from system to system, the result is that electronic documents can be freely passed between systems. We can now be a little more precise about the notion of an electronic document: it contains electronic or machine-readable text with descriptive markup codes which may be used to determine the rendition and other usages of the document. Before we go on to give an idea of how this can be exploited for MT, it may be worth a brief description of the standard descriptive markup: SGML (Standardised General Markup Language) which is specified by the International Standards Organization.

It is our belief that in the next few years no serious commercial MT system will be supplied without some means of handling SGML. SGML specifies that, ordinarily, text will be marked up in the way shown in the last example above, i.e. with document elements surrounded by their names in angle brackets. An office memo marked up in SGML might look like the example below. In addition to the actual text, various pairs of SGML tags delimiting the memo elements can be seen here. The memo as a whole starts with `<Memo>` and ends with `</Memo>` (where / indicates the closing delimiter). In between the Memo tag pair we find the sub-elements of the memo, also marked-up with paired tags (`<To>... </To>`, `<From>.. </From>`, `<Body>... <P>..</P>...</Body>`).

The relationship between SGML tags, and the way text is actually rendered is given by an association table, such a table might say, e.g. that the body of a memo should be separated from the previous part by a horizontal line.

The tagging principles of SGML are intended to extend to very complex and highly structured documents. Imposing such a structure not only allows very fine, and flexible control of how documents are printed, it can also allow easy access to and manipulation of information in documents, and straightforward consistency checking. One thing the SGML standard does not do is try to specify a standard inventory of all possible document elements. Users are perfectly free to define their own document types and to specify the elements in those documents. SGML provides a special method of doing this known as a Document Type Definition (DTD).

A DTD is a sort of formal grammar specifying all such relations in a particular type of document. For example, such a grammar might say that all Memos contain a To element followed by a From element followed by a Body element, which itself contains at least one Paragraph followed by zero or more Paragraphs. This means that a Memo has the following sort of DTD (grossly simplified):

```
Memo → To, From, Body
Body → Paragraph, Paragraph*
```

Using a DTD has several advantages:

1 The DTD makes sure that documents are truly portable between different SGML document systems; the document system reads the accompanying DTD to find out what sort of elements will be in the document and how they will be arranged with respect to each other. Thus, the document processing system knows what to expect when it encounters a document which is an instance of a certain DTD.

2 It ensures that documents of a particular type (e.g. user manuals) are always structurally consistent with each other. It suffices to define a DTD for the class of user manuals and then the SGML document processing system will ensure that all documents produced by that DTD will indeed have the same overall structure. In short, DTDs help to promote a certain rigour which is extremely desirable in technical documentation.

3 The use of DTDs in document preparation allows authors to deal directly with the content of texts whilst having little or no direct contact with the actual markup used. What happens with the usual sort of SGML system is that there is a window offering the author a choice of document entities appropriate for the document she is preparing or revising. This list of document entities is obtained by reading the DTD for the document. For example, in a memo, there will be a choice of To, From, and Body. The author clicks on the appropriate element

and the markup is entered into the text (perhaps invisibly). When actually typing in the Body, the choice is narrowed down to Paragraph. Whilst this is not particularly interesting for simple documents like memos, it is clear that it would be immensely useful in constructing complex documents, and in document retrieval.

With this general idea of Electronic Documents and markup, we can look at how an MT system can exploit the fact that texts are represented in this way.

SGML Markup and MT Input

An MT system should only attempt to translate things that are translatable. Suppose that some text contains the acronym 'MAT', which refers to a company called 'Machine Aided Translation Ltd'. Clearly the correct translation of this is either just MAT again or some new acronym that reflects the translation of the underlying name — perhaps TAO in French, being the acronym for Traduction Assist´ee par Ordinateur, which itself is the translation of Machine Aided Translation. What is unquestionably incorrect is a translation of the form pallaison, this being the sort of mat that a cat might sit on.

The reader may think that the MT system ought to have spotted that MAT cannot be a standard concrete noun because it is capitalised; but many MT systems routinely ignore capitals because they need to recognise ordinary words which can appear with an initial capital letter at the start of a sentence. The way to deal with this sort of problem is to ensure that acronyms are recognised as a particular class of text elements and marked up as such. This might be done (a) either by the author when the text is being created or (b) by special tools used before translation which help translators to find acronyms and the like and mark them up accordingly.

For example, a specialised search and replace tool inside the document pre-editor could look for all sequences of capitalised words and, after querying the translator to check whether a particular candidate sequence really is an acronym, insert the appropriate markers in the text. The point is that once the text is marked up, the MT system is in a much better situation to know that it is dealing with an untranslatable acronym and to treat it accordingly. Similarly, consider figures and diagrams in a document. These consist usually of pictorial material, which is untranslatable, and a translatable text caption which characterises the pictorial material.

Recognising the markup tags which indicate that the following material in the document is pictorial, the MT system can simply ignore everything until it encounters another tag telling it that it is about to see the caption, which it can translate as a normal piece of text. Equally, it is easy to ask the MT system to translate (say) just a single chapter, because the markup in the document will clearly identify the piece of text that constitutes the chapter. Markup is thus a powerful tool in controlling the MT process.

DTDs are particularly useful in MT. Some MT systems keep a copy of each sentence they have already encountered together with its translation (the post-edited version, if available). This habit is known in the industry as Translation Memory. Over the years, MT vendors have found that in some organizations much of the translation workload consists of entirely re-translating revised editions of technical manuals. These revised editions may contain as much as 90% of the material that was already present in the previous edition — and which was already translated and post-edited.

Hence automatically recognising sentences already translated and retrieving the post-edited translation — as the Translation Memory technique allows — results in a

90% reduction in post-editing costs (and an enormous increase in the overall speed of the translation process). This is clearly very significant. However, these sort of performance improvements are really the result of a defective doc-umentation process. The problem is that the organization paying to have the translation done is not keeping proper track of which parts of a revised document really are different from the original version.

Clearly only new or altered material really needs to be even considered for translation.Within the SGML standard it is possible to add features to text elements to record when they were last altered, by whom and so on. This version control information can be maintained by the document system and it allows the user to extract revised elements. Indeed, the principle can be extended so that earlier versions of a given revised element are also kept, allowing the user to reconstruct any previous version of a document at any point. The result of exercising proper version control in documentation is that only new elements for which there are no existing translations will be submitted to the translation process.

In this way, the document processing system takes some of the burden otherwise carried by the MT system (viz, the 'Translation Memory' facility). Another advantage of using DTDs in MT involves generalizing the notion of a document slightly, to introduce the notion of a 'multilingual document'. In SGML, this is largely a matter of altering the DTDs of monolingual document types. Take the Memo example: we can get a multilingual version by specifying that there is a copy of each document element for each language. Here is a revised (and still simplified) Memo DTD for two languages:

```
Memo → To, From, Body

Body → Paragraph, Paragraph*

Paragraph → Paragraph-L1, Paragraph-L2
```

There are now two types of Paragraph — Paragraphs in language one and Paragraphs in language 2. Each Paragraph element will contain one language 1 paragraph followed by one language 2 paragraph. (There are no language specific To and From elements because it is assumed that they contain only proper names). This sort of technique can be generalised to allow a document to carry text in arbitrarily many languages. Though this allows a document to contain text for more than one language, it does not require it — document elements can be empty — this would be the case for target language elements where the source element has not yet been translated.

The important thing to understand here is that just because the simple multilingual DTD we have described 'interleaves' the elements for different languages (we have a paragraph for L1 followed by the corresponding paragraph for L2, etc.), this does not mean that we have to view the document that way. For example, a Memo in English, French and German can be viewed on the screen of a document processing system with all the English paragraphs, printed together, and the French paragraphs printed alongside, with the German paragraphs not shown at all.

Part of the flexibility in the rendition of a marked-up document is that the text content of classes of elements can be hidden or shown at will. In practical terms, this means that a translator editing a multilingual document will have considerable flexibility in choosing the way in which that document is presented (on screen or on paper) and in choosing the type of element she wishes to see. Turning back to the MT case ETRANS takes the German text and then makes available the English translation in the multilingual document.

It should now be much clearer how this works. Translatable elements from the source text are passed to the ETRANS system which then translates them. The translated text is then placed under the corresponding target language text elements (which, up that point, have been entirely empty of text). So far as is linguistically possible, the structure of the document is preserved. In summary, it should be clear that the general idea of the Electronic Document is important within the context of MT and can make a considerable contribution to the successful integration of MT within the office environment.

Controlled Languages

The notion of controlled languages is a form of language usage restricted by grammar and vocabulary rules. The original idea arose during the 1930s, when a number of influential linguists and scholars devoted considerable effort to establishing a 'minimal' variety of English, a variety specifically designed to make English accessible to and usable by the largest possible number of people world wide. Basic English, as it was called, differed from previous attempts to construct universal languages in that it was a perfectly well-formed part of English, rather than some entirely artificial or hybrid construction such as Esperanto.

One of the central ideas of the Basic English movement was that the number of general-purpose words needed for writing anything from a simple letter of receipt through to a major speech on the world economic situation could be a few hundred rather than the 75 000 upward available to skilled native speakers. This lexical economy was to be achieved in part by using 'operator verbs' with the set of nouns and adjectives to stand in for the vast number of derived verbs which are frequently used.

For example, whereas in ordinary English we might write The disc controller design was perfected over numerous revisions, Basic English would say... was made perfect..., where make is one of the operator verbs and perfect one of the licensed Basic English adjectives. The authors of Basic English explicitly recognised that the dictionary would need to be extended with special terminology for scientific and technical writing. However, even if a text contained terminology specific to a certain subject field, the general language component of the text could perfectly well be accommodated within Basic English.

The important point remains that, for writing in a particular subject field, no more is needed than the Basic English dictionary together with a (relatively small) technical vocabulary for that field. The idea was later taken on by English-language based (predominantly North American) corporations marketing capital goods on a world-wide basis. Rather than try to translate engine manuals and the like into every possible language that might be required, it was assumed that if they were written with sufficient care and attention, they could be read fairly easy by service engineers and mechanics with limited English skills.

Although controlled languages were introduced partly to avoid or reduce human translation costs, two important additional benefits were discovered. First, the readability and clarity of a controlled language technical text often seems better than uncontrolled texts — even for native English readers. Second, controlled languages produce better results with MT than uncontrolled languages. The reasons for controlled languages' superior MT performance are easy to understand. First, the restricted vocabulary means that fewer words need to be added to the MT system dictionaries and more effort can be put into getting the entries which are required right.

Second, the grammar component of the system can be tailored to handle all and only those constructions which are licensed by the controlled language specification, a specification which excludes the most difficult and ambiguous constructions anyway. A flavour of what is involved can be obtained by looking at the writing rules given above and the dictionary excerpt on page 149, which are based on those of PACE, the controlled English used by the UK Engineering company Perkins Engines.As will be clear from the dictionary excerpt, the general principle is 'one word, one meaning', for example, the only use of the verb advise is 'to give advice'.

Using a restricted pool of words and terms also means that the system dictionaries can be tailored (by the MT supplier or responsible translator) to cover exactly that set of words and their translations. Being consistent about the use of terms will also help to improve the overall consistency and quality of the texts being translated. After all, one of the simplest and most direct benefits of MT for technical texts is that terms are always translated consistently because they are simply looked up in an electronic bilingual term dictionary.

In general, it can be seen that the rules are mainly advice on constructions that should be avoided, usually because they lead to ambiguity. The rules for controlled languages tend to be stylistic guidelines rather than hard and fast grammar specifications. In general, much of the success of controlled languages as corporate language tools stems from the emphasis placed on critical analysis of the text and precise presentation of ideas. This is particularly apparent in the first example on page 151, which illustrates the dramatic effect of using a controlled version of English.

It is not particularly difficult to train people to write controlled language text i.e. text which generally observes some set of fairly simple writing rules. For example, the Xerox corporation currently offers its technical writers a one-day course in writing with MCE (Multinational Customised English, a Xerox proprietary language). British Aerospace teaches the rudiments of Simplified English (a general purpose technical English for the international aerospace industry) in a few fairly short training sessions.

Sublanguage MT

The term sublanguage refers to the specialized language used (predominantly for communication between experts) in certain fields of knowledge, for example, the language of weather reports, stockmarket reports, the language of some kinds of medical discussion, the language of aeronautical engineering. Specialized vocabulary is one characteristic of such 'languages' (they typically contain words not known to the non-specialist and also words used in different or more precise ways). However sublanguages are also often characterised by special or restricted grammatical patterns.

In MT, it is quite common to use the term sublanguage rather loosely to refer not just to such a specialized language, but to its use in a particular type of text (e.g. installation manuals, instruction booklets, diagnostic reports, learned articles), or with a particular communicative purpose (communication between experts, giving instructions to non-experts, etc). The chief attraction of sublanguage and text type restriction to MT researchers is the promise of improved output, without the need to artificially restrict the input.

Restricting the coverage to texts of particular types in certain subject domains will allow one to profit from regularities and restrictions in syntactic form and lexical content. This may be important enough to permit significant simplification of the architecture, and certainly leads to a reduction in the overall coverage required. Of course, the language of meteorological reports is special in happening to combine a rather small vocabulary with a simple, telegraphic style of writing.

Nonetheless, a simplification of lexical and possibly syntactic coverage can be expected in less extreme cases. To give an example with respect to lexical coverage, it is reported that 114 of the 125 occurrences of the verb to match in a computer software manual translate into the

Japanese icchisuru-suru, which is listed as one of the less frequent of the 15 translations given in a small-size English-Japanese dictionary. In the extract from a corpus of telecommunications text given below, traffic always corresponds to the French trafic and never to circulation (which applies only to road traffic).

Moreover the dictionary writer can safely ignore the meaning of both trafic and traffic concerning dealings in illegal merchandise ('drug traffic'). Also, for an increasing number of sublanguages one can rely on the availability of a termbank (an on-line (multilingual) terminological dictionary) defining and stating equivalences for many of the technical terms that will be encountered. This greatly eases the job of dictionary construction. Such examples can be multiplied almost at will.

As for syntactic coverage, examples of instruction manuals and other forms of informative documentation typically share a number of common features. There will probably be no idioms, and a restricted set of sentential patterns. Another common feature is the relatively simple temporal dimension of the text, e.g. predominant use of the simple present. There is also the common occurrence of enumeration as a form of conjunction, usually either numbered or inset by dashes, etc. Some of these features can be seen by comparing the examples of English and French given below, which are drawn from a corpus of texts about Telecommunications.

All are of great benefit to the developer or user of an MT system. For the developer, they mean that there are fewer problems of ambiguity, and development effort can be concentrated on a smaller range of constructions. For the user, this should mean that better coverage is obtained, and that the system performs better. It is not, of course, the case that expository texts in different languages always exploit the same devices for a particular communicative purpose.

The following extracts from the same corpus show that English and French differ in their use of impersonal constructions, with French favouring such constructions with the impersonal subject pronoun il ('it') far more in this type of text than English does. But even in these cases, it is generally easier to choose the correct translation, simply because the range of possibilities in such texts is smaller.

(1) a. In this framework, the progressive evolution of the earth segment should be considered. Dans ce contexte, il convient de prendre en compte l'´evolution progressive du secteur terrien.

(2) a. Setting up a new satellite system, which may be either a regional system with the participation of a group of countries, or a purely national (domestic) system, is obviously much more difficult than using an existing system:

Il est manifestement beaucoup plus difficile de mettre en place un nouveau syst'eme 'a satellites (syst'eme regional auquel participe un groupe de pays ou syst'eme purement national) que d'utiliser un syst'eme existant:

(3) a. Simultaneously, arrangements should be made for recruitment and training of staff for installation, operation and maintenance.

b. En meme temps, il convient de prendre des dispositions pour le recrutement et la formation du personnel qui sera charge de l'installation, de l'exploitation et de la maintenance.

Text type can strongly influence translation, not just because certain syntactic constructions are favoured (e.g. conjunction by enumeration), but also by giving special meanings to certain forms. An example of how the text type can be useful in determining translationa l equivalents is the translation of infinitive verb forms from French or German into English. Infinitives normally correspond to English infinitives, but are usually translated as English imperatives in instructional texts. Thus, in a printer manual one would see (4b) as the translation of (4a), rather than the literal translation.

(4) a. Richtige Spannung einstellen 'correct voltage to set'

b. Set correct voltage

(5) a. Executer les commandes 'to execute the commands'

b. Execute the commands

Thus, concentration on a sublanguage not only restricts the vocabulary and the number of source and target language constructions to be considered, it can also restrict the number of possible target translations. Given the potential that sublanguages provide for improvements in the quality of output of MT systems, and the fact that most commercial institutions do in fact have their major translation needs in restricted areas, it is not surprising that many research prototypes concentrate on restricted input in various ways, and that the design of tools and resources supporting sublanguage analysis is a major area of research.

15

Report Format and Final Production

Formatting Guidelines

Some general formatting guidelines are given below:

— Use 1- or 1-1/2-inch margins for all four margins of the report. You might want to use a 1-1/2-inch margin at the top and 1-inch margins for the left, right, and bottom.

— Use a 1-1/2-inch left margin if your binding uses a lot of space (for example, brad-type binders that require 2- or 3-hole punch).

— Generally use doublespaced typing except in those areas where singlespacing is shown (for example, in the transmittal letter, descriptive abstract, figure titles, short vertical lists, and items in the information-sources list).

— Use one side of the paper only.

Component of Formal Reports

This section examine Each component of the formal report and points out the key requirements in terms of content, design, and format. Remember that these are requirements, or "specifications." Much of the work that professional technical writers do is governed by specifications. Just as an electric component much be built according to certain design specifications, so must most technical documents such as instructions manuals, reference books, and so on. Your job, like any technical writer's, is to stay as close to the specifications as you possibly can.

Covers and Label

Your final report should use some sort of cover and label. The best is the plastic spiral binding that you can have done at most copy shops. It uses only a quarter-inch of the left margin, and the bound report lies flat when open. The least expensive binding is the type for which you punch holes in the left margin and fix the pages in the folder with brads.

Loose-leaf, ring binders are generally too large and bulky-also the pages tear. Copy shops offer other kinds of binding that work well also. However, avoid the clear or colored plastic ones with the plastic sleeve that fits on the left side-not only is it grade-schoolish, it's aggravating to use. As for the label, the best option is to design your own and print it out on an ordinary sheet of paper, then take it to the copy shop and have it copied onto the cover of your choice. Adhesive labels are okay-but you have to buy hundreds of them and then find a typewriter to type them.

Transmittal letter

The transmittal letter basically says "here's that report we agreed I'd write!" Notice that it mentions the contract date, briefly discusses the purposes and main contents of the report, and then closes with a polite suggestion to get in touch after the recipient has had time to review the report. (Notice that the middle paragraph is very repetitious of the descriptive abstract and the introduction-that's okay. Reports are designed to accommodate multiple entry points by readers.)

— *Title page and descriptive abstract*: At the bottom of the title page is the descriptive abstract. See the section on descriptive abstracts for further details.

- *Table of contents*: The table of contents (TOC) lists the headings from the body of the report and the page numbers on which they occur. It is not required to list all headings. This TOC could have excluded all third-level headings and fit on one page.
- *List of Figures*: In the list of figures, you list all of the titles for figures and tables in your report. If any title is too long, trim it to a meaningful portion.
- Abstract
- Body of the report

Page with headings and graphics: In the body of your report, be sure to use the standard format for headings for lists and for graphics. If you are writing instructions, don't forget to use the standard format for special notices.

Appendixes: The appendix is a good place to put information that just will not fit in the main body of the report, but still needs to be in the report. For example, big tables of data, large maps, forms used in an organization, or background discussion-these are good candidates for the appendix. Notice that each one is given a letter (A, B, C, and so on).

Information sources: Remember to put all information sources in this list, including nonprinted, nonpublished ones. For style and format of these entries, see the section on documentation.

Page-numbering style: Page numbering in technical reports may seem a little peculiar. However, it is pretty much the same style used generally in traditional publishing.

1. All pages within the front and back covers are numbered (except for the transmittal letter); but the page number is not always displayed.
2. All pages coming before page 1 of the introduction use lowercase Roman numerals.

3. All pages beginning with page 1 of the introduction use with Arabic numerals.

4. Page numbers are not displayed on the transmittal letter, title page, first page of the table of contents, page 1 of the introduction, and the appendix divider page.

5. There are several choices of pagination style for the main-text pages:

   — Center page numbers at the bottom (halfway between the last text line and the bottom edge of the paper).

   — Place page numbers in the top right corner (on the right margin, halfway between the top text line and the top edge of the paper). Do not display page numbers on any page with a centered (first-level) heading (display it centered at the bottom).

6. Some word-processing software causes problems in implementing these pagination guidelines; let your instructor know.

Final Production

Once you have your final draft as polished as you can get it, you are ready to "package" it for final production. Here are the steps:

1. Make a good printout (or final typing) of your report, on good paper, using fresh print supplier (ribbon, toner, cartridge, whatever you printer or typewriter uses). Remember to design and type or print your cover label.

2. Make sure your graphics are good quality. If they are, tape them down onto the pages. Make sure they fit neatly within the margins-top and bottom, left and right.

3. Make sure all the components are in place and everything looks okay.

4. Head for a good copy shop-there, get a good photocopy of your text pages. Check to see how the pages with taped-in graphics look. If they are not right, ask a copy-shop person for help.

5. Now select the cover and have the label you design printed on it. Most shops have numerous colors and thicknesses of covers to choose from.

6. Finally, get the report with its cover bound. The plastic spiral binding works great. There are other bindings that work nicely too. Remember, though-no clear plastic cover with those plastic sleeves on the left side!

16

Power-revision Techniques

Writing teachers tend not to do much with this sort of stuff in their classrooms because it's just plain old hard and tedious. Yet, if we were to find a way to make these revision concepts and techniques easier to learn, practice, and apply, we might have achieved one of the most important breakthroughs in the teaching of writing. This stuff can become second nature rather quickly though. The way you write and the way you review what you write will change. You'll start operating-and not even be fully aware of it-with this stuff in mind.

Therefore, if we had the proper materials, the proper equipment for you to work out on for several weeks (some sort of verbal NordicTrac), these concepts and techniques would become nearly second nature to you and really give a big boost to this most important area of your writing.

Structure-level Revision

For lack of a better phrase, "structure-level revision" refers to the techniques you can use to improve the content of a document, make it better organized, and facilitate readers' ability to follow and understand it. At this level, we're not tinkering with commas or subject-verb agreement-we're tossing around whole paragraphs, adding whole new sentences, deleting chunks of useless text, reorganizing sections, and adding various kinds of signals to make things easier to follow. Specifically, this section on structure-level revision techniques covers the following:

— Contents

— Structure

— Organization

— Topic sentences and overviews

— Transitions

Check Contents

One of the most important ways you can review a rough draft is to check the contents. All the good transitions, good organization, and clear sentence structure in the world can't help a report that doesn't have the right information. Information in a report can be "wrong" in several ways:

— It can be missing altogether: for example, imagine that somebody wrote a report on "virtual communities" but never bothered to define what that term means. It would be tough going from the start of that report.

— It's there but not enough of it: take the same example-imagine that the writer only made a few vague statements about virtual communities. What was needed was at least a paragraph on the subject, if not a full-blown 3- or 4-page section.

— It's there but at the wrong level for the audience: It's also possible to pitch information at the wrong level in terms of readers' knowledge, background, or needs. Imagine that the writer did include a 3-page section on data caching but written for the product developer (an "expert" audience) when the report was really intended for nonspecialists.

If you can get a sense of how information is inadequate in a report rough draft, you should be well on your way to knowing what specifically to do to revise. One useful brainstorming tool is to think in terms of types of content. Use the following questions to review your rough draft for the types of information to add or change:

— *Definitions*: Are there key terms in your report that need to be defined? Is one of those terms so important that it needs a full section for adequate definition? Most terms can be defined in a sentence or two at the point they first occur, but some terms may be so important to the report and so complex that they need a whole section (one or more paragraphs) to define.

— *Description*: Are there objects, mechanisms, places, animals, even people that need to be described? If you are comparing different models of some sort of new equipment, should you describe them physically first? Can you divide the thing into parts, components, or characteristics and describe each separately? Consider whether to work this description into the existing discussion or to make it its own separate section.

— *Process discussion*: Are there processes in your report that you should discuss in detail? They may be either natural processes (those occurring in nature) or human-controlled processes (those that are initiated, controlled, or performed by people). Again, as with description, you may be able to work this extended process explanation into the existing discussion, or you may want to put it in a separate section of its own.

— *Comparisons*: Would comparison to similar or more familiar things be helpful? Would analogies help-extended discussion of similarities between your topic and something familiar. Are evaluative comparisons needed in your report-in other words, comparisons that lead to a decision or recommendation?

— *Division into categories*: Are there subcategories associated with your topic? Would discussing them improve your discussion? Consider an extended discussion of the categories-with an introductory paragraph that explains the principle of the classification then separate paragraphs on each of the categories.

— *Location within a category*: Would it help readers to understand your discussion better if you located the topic in one of several categories (for example, by discussing whether some new computer model is a laptop, notebook, or subnotebook)?

— *Causal discussion*: Should you include an extended discussion of the causes of some situation related to your topic? Should you include an extended discussion of the effects (consequences, results) of some situation related to your topic? If you use the extended approach, see whether you can separate the discussion of each cause or effect into a section of its own.

— *Examples*: In technical discussions, examples are almost always in order. Examples can be worked into the existing text, or you may want to see about creating a separate section for extended discussion of an example.

— *Analogies*: Analogies, as mentioned above, are extended comparisons. You compare your technical topic to something very familiar (for example, a computer to a typewriter-although how familiar is the typewriter any more?).

— *Historical background*: Can you discuss the history, people, events related to your topic? Would this discussion help readers better understand your discussion or help you better achieve your writing purpose?

— *Instructions*: Are readers looking to your report for instructions on building, assembling, operating, or repairing something.

— *Narrative*: Is there some event associated with your topic that needs to be discussed. Narrative is different from process discussion, mentioned earlier: narrative discusses a one-time series of events; process discusses a routine, repeated, or repeatable series of events. If you do need to include narrative, consider putting it in its own separate section.

— *Content based on typical reports*: One other way to brainstorm about the contents of a report is to review the typical contents of the type of report you are writing. For example, if you are writing a laboratory report, there are certain expected contents-make sure you've included them, or at least the ones that apply.

There are two ways of looking at the organization of information in a document: one, covered in the next section, involves looking at the sequence of chunks of information, seeing if they are in the right order. Another has to do with levels of information. You can look at the sentences or paragraphs in a rough draft and see that some sentences go to a deeper level of discussion on the topic than others. Other sentences act like the framework upon which those deeper-level sentences depend. By looking at structure in this way, you not only check its organization but also get a lot of good ideas about how to improve the content of the text.

You can view your writing in these structural terms at any level. Instead of sentences, you can think in terms of paragraphs, whole groups of paragraphs, or even large sections of writing. How can you use this kind of structural view of your writing? First, it is obviously a good way to check for organization. More powerfully, however, this approach enables you to sense what else you might say about your topic.

Check Organization

If you have the right information in a report, at least you've got all the "right stuff" available for readers. However, it may still not be adequately organized-like when you've just moved and everything is a mess or still in boxes. You need two essential skills for reviewing the organization of a rough draft:

— Identifying the topic of chunks of information at various levels. To assess the organization of a string of paragraphs, you start by thinking of a word or phrase to identify the topic of each paragraphs-in other words, get a handle on each one. Then you stand back from those words or phrases, considering whether they are in the right sequence. However, that's only one level. You can also look within an individual paragraph for its organization. In this case, you identify the topic of each sentence and consider the sequencing of those sentences.

— Choosing the best sequence for chunks of information. Once you know the topic of each of the chunks of information (at whatever level you are investigating), then you can decide whether they are in the right sequence. This decision involves knowing the common sequencing patterns; here are some examples:

  — *General -> specific*: One of the most comon ways to organize is to arrange chunks of information from general to specific. For example, defining all solar collectors is a more general discussion than discussing the different types of solar collectors. And describing the operation of a specific type of solar collector is even less general.

  — *Simple, basic -> complex*: Another way to arrange units of a discussion is to begin with the simple, basic, fundamental ones and then move on to the more complex and technical.

  — *Thing-at-rest -> thing-in-motion*: Another organization pattern involves first describing the thing (as if in a photograph), then discussing its operation or process (as if in a video). This approach might work well for a discussion of a fuel-injection system.

— *Spatial movement*: If you are describing the physical details of something, you might want to use some pattern of physical movement, for example, top to bottom, left to right, or outside to inside.

— *Temporal movement*: One of the most common patterns is based on movement through time; arrange the discussion of events in relation to the temporal sequence.

— *Concept -> application of the concept, examples*: A common organizational pattern is to discuss a concept in general terms then discuss an application of it.

— *Data -> conclusions*: Another means of organizing information is to present data (observations, experimental data, survey results) then move on to the conclusions that can be drawn from that data.

— *Problem, question -> solution, answer*: You can also organize information by first discussing a problem or raising a question then moving on to the solution or answer.

— *Simplified version->detailed version*: A useful way to explain technical matters to nonspecialists is to begin by discussing a simplified version of the thing, establish a solid understanding of it, then go right back and explain it all again but this time laying on the technical detail thick and heavy!

— *Most important -> least important*: A more "rhetorical" method of organization is to begin with the most important, the most eye-catching, the most dramatic information first then move on to information that is progressively less so.

— *Most convincing -> least convincing*: Similarly, you can start with the most convincing argument for your position-to get everybody's attention-then move on to less and less convincing ones.

These are just a few possibilities. When the aim is informative, you arrange information so that you ensure that readers understand the basics before moving onto the complicated, technical stuff. When the aim is persuasive, you arrange things to maximize the persuasive effect on the readers, for example, by putting the strongest arguments first. And in any case, you avoid mixing these approaches-for example, throwing out some data, then stating a few conclusions, and then doing this back and forth in a haphazard way.

Strengthen Topic Sentences

One of the best things you can do is go back through a rough draft and check to see if you can insert topic sentences and overviews at key points. When we write, we're not normally sure exactly where a paragraph or section is going in terms of its content and logic. Once it has "gotten there," it is often necessary to go back to the beginning and add some sort of overview or modify what's already there to make the overview clearer.

Readers need to know where they are going in a report, what's coming up next, and for that matter where they've just been. Having an overview in a report is like having a map when you're in a new city. Topic sentences and overviews offer a perspective on what's where: the topic, the subtopics, its relation to the previous section and to the document as a whole.

Strengthen Transitions

You can have the right information in a report and have it organized properly, but something important can still go wrong. Readers can miss the "flow" of the ideas, have a hard time sensing how the chunks of information are related or connected to each other. What readers need is continuous guidance-which is what you the writer provide. And what you use to provide that guidance is called transitions-various devices that help readers along through a document. There is (or certainly should be) a logic that connects every sentence in a document and that dictates a certain sequence to those sentences.

Your sense of that logic enables you to put the various chunks of information in a report in the proper order. However, readers may have trouble at times seeing that logic. Transitions emphasize that logic. It's not that the connecting point between every pair of information chunks requires some full-blown transition-just the ones that readers are likely to have trouble getting through. Usually, as writers, we almost unconsciously supply the transitional devices that guide readers along. But sometimes we forget, or sometimes a connection that seems obvious to us is hard for readers to see.

Then we need to work particularly hard to make the connection apparent. Once you've identified problem points in your rough draft where better transitions are needed, the next step is to analyze each problem point and find the transition that will improve the connection. To do this, you need to understand something about how transitions operate and what choices you have among them. First, in principle, a transition is a signal that shows how a preceding chunk of information is logically related to a current or upcoming chunk of information. It looks backwards and looks forward at the same time.

People who have studied the way communication, in particular, writing, works have identified these kinds of basic logic that knit ideas together:

— *Additive*: One idea can be added to another; information can simply be added to other information within a paragraph. Additive transitional words and phrases include and, moreover, as well as, too, in addition to, furthermore, also, and additionally.

— *Narrative, chronological, temporal*: One idea can follow, precede, or occur simultaneously with another. Narrative transitional words and phrases include then, next, after, before, since, subsequently, following, later, as soon as, as, when, while, during, until, and once.

— *Contrastive, comparative*: Two ideas can be compared to each other to show differences or similarities. Contrastive transitional words and phrases include but, on the other hand, unlike, as opposed to, than, although, though, instead, and similarly.

— *Alternative*: Two ideas can act as alternatives or substitutes for each other. Alternative transitional words and phrases include either, or, nor, on the other hand, however, neither, and otherwise.

— *Causal*: One idea can be the cause or the result (effect, consequence, etc.) of another. Causal transitional words and phrases include thus, then, unless, subsequently, therefore, because, consequently, as a result, if, in order to/that, for, and so.

— *Illustrative*: One idea can be an example or an illustration of another. Illustrative transitional words and phrases include for example, for instance, to illustrate, and as an example.

— *Repetitive, reiterative*: To ensure clarity, an idea can be restated or repeated using other, perhaps more familiar, words. Repetitive transitional words and phrases include in other words, in short, that is, stated simply, and to put it another way.

— *Spatial, physical*: The things referred to by one statement can have a spatial relationship to another thing referred to by another statement. The logic connecting the two statements can be spatial in nature. Typically, prepositions indicate such logic: for example, under, beside, on top of, next to, behind, and so on.

It takes a surprising amount of brain power to construct a transition: you must know the topic of the preceding chunk of information, the topic of the current or upcoming one, the logic that connects them. Then, with that in mind, you must pick out the transitional device that you think will best guide the reader across that juncture between the two chunks of information.

— *Transitional words*: The easiest to spot are words like "but," "however," "on the other hand," "therefore," "for example," "in other word," "in addition," and so on. These specifically mark the logic as contrastive, alternative, causal, illustrative, additive, and so on, which we looked at in the preceding section.

— *Repeated key words*: Strangely enough, simply repeating the key word, the word that is the focus of topic of the discussion is also a transitional device-but not a very strong one of course. You can actually improve the flow of a piece of writing by working on the way you repeat the key words. As writers, for some reason, we feel compelled to vary word choice.

However, this can lead to problems when it involves the main topic or subtopics. After all, if you suddenly start calling a "diskette" a "disk," people may wonder if you're talking about something different. Therefore, in a technical context, it's often a better choice to use the same words, even at the risk of sounding a bit repetitive. Where the repeated key words occur in a sentence can also affect the ease by which readers follow your discussion. If you bury the key word at the end of the sentence, it takes readers just that much longer to reach the signal that shows them the connection.

— *Pronouns*: Pronouns do the same thing as repeated key words, only more efficiently. In a previous example, the pronoun "it" instead of repeating "Peugeot." Of course, the risk you run with pronouns is that readers won't be able to figure out what the pronoun refers to. Pronouns like "it," "this," "which," "that," "they," "them," and the like are vulnerable to this problem. When this happens, the summary transition can help strengthen the transition.

— *Summary transitions*: At key points in writing, particularly at the beginning or end of paragraphs or sections, you'll see a phrase, sometimes accompanied by a pronoun, that summarizes the preceding discussion. In the same sentence, a statement will be made about that summary phrase-typically this phrase will kick off the upcoming discussion, and do so in a way that the reader sees the connection between what came before and what is coming next. While this may sound like a device to use at the beginning or end of a paragraph, you'll actually see it right in the middle of long and complex paragraphs.

— *Review-preview transitions*: The most powerful transitional device you can use is the type that summarizes the topic of the preceding chunk of information into a short phrase, does the same thing for the upcoming chunk of information, finds the appropriate transitional word, and then throws all these elements together into a sentence or two. You'd use this device at those major bridge points in reports, between large chunks of information-for example, between one 7-page section and a 9-page section that follows it.

— *Parallel phrasing*: Another transitional device-more of a gimmick actually-is to use the same phrasing in a series of sentences, each one of which adds another detail to some topic. In other words, parallel phrasing is limited to situations where additive logic is involved.

Paragraph Length and Contents

One last way to review your rough draft at the structure level is to check how you have defined the paragraph breaks. Paragraphs are odd creatures-some scholars of writing believe they don't exist and are just arbitrary break points that writers toss in whenever and wherever they damn well please. Sorry-in technical writing, the paragraph is a key player in the battle for clarity and comprehension. Although not always possible, paragraphs should occur where there is some shift in topic or subtopic or some shift in the way a topic is being discussed.

On a doublespaced full page of writing, look for at least one to two paragraph breaks-there's nothing magical about that average so don't treat it as if it were law. Just take a second look at those long paragraphs, and check for the possibility of paragraph breaks. And, while you're reviewing the paragraphing of your rough draft, take another look at the contents of those paragraphs: are there things that don't belong?

Sentence-level Revision

You've probably heard plenty of times that writing should be lean, mean, clear, direct, succinct, active, and so on. This is one of those self-evident truths-why would anyone set out to write any other way? But what does that really mean, what do sentences look like that are not that way, what sorts of things are wrong with them, and how do you fix them?

Sentences do have ways of becoming flabby, redundant, wordy, unclear, indirect, passive, and just plain old hard to understand. Even so, they remain grammatically "correct"-all their subjects and verbs agree, the commas are in the right places, the words are spelled correctly. Still, these sentences are far more difficult to read than any sentence with just a comma problem.

The following sections can't pretend to cover all of the ways sentences can go bad at this higher level, but they do cover seven of the most common problems and shows you ways of fixing them. And knowing these seven will probably enable you to spot all the others we have not trapped and labeled yet. Specifically, here is what is covered:

— Weak be verbs

— Overnominalization ("noun stacks")

— Redundant phrasing

— Weak use of expletives (there is, it is)

— Weak use of the passive voice

— Subject-verb mismatch

— Sentence length

Revise Weak be-verbs

One of the big culprits that cause weak, indirect writing is the use of the be verb as the main verb. That's not to say that the be verb should never be used as the main verb, just that there are cases where doing so makes for weak writing. Look at the following examples of this problem-they are not that hard to spot. Then look at the revisions-notice how a noun (often one ending in -ion) has been converted into a verb. That's how to fix this problem-find a noun to convert into an active verb, and then rebuild the sentence upon it.

Revise Noun Stacks

Another common sentence-style problem involves piling up nouns in a phrase. The effect is similar being hit in the head with a large blunt object. Again, take a look at the examples of this problem, which are also not hard to spot, and at the revisions. When you revise a "noun stack," you unpack or unstack the nouns into clauses and phrases.

Revise Redundant Phrasing

Redundancy in writing can come about from these three sources (but there are probably plenty more):

— Wordy set phrases (where a 4- to 5-word phrase and be chopped to a 1- to 2-word phrase with no loss of meaning): for example, "in view of the fact that"-it can be reduced to "since" or "because."

— Obvious qualifiers (where a word is implicit in the word it modifies): phrases like "anticipate in advance," "completely finish," or "important essentials" are examples of obvious qualifiers-we know that already.

— Scattershot phrasing (where two or more synonyms are compounded): compounds like "thoughts and ideas" (what's the difference?) or "actions and behavior" (if there is a difference between these two, does the writer mean to use it?).

Revise Weak Expletives

If you were around for Watergate, the term "expletive" means something specific to you (in the tapes and transcripts of Nixon's staff, many expletives had to be "deleted"). However, the term expletive refers to variations of there is and it is. This is not to say that it is always wrong to use these phrases in sentences, but they can easily be misused or overused. Like redundant phrasing, they add more words than are needed, and more words blunt the meaning, create a fog around the sense of a sentence.

Revise Weak Passive-voice Sentences

One of the all-time worst offenders for creating unclear, wordy, indirect writing is the passive-voice construction. It's easy enough to convert a sentence from active voice to passive voice, and back again:

Active: The student wrote the report.
Passive: The report was written by the student.

However, the passive voice can be a shifty operator-it can cover up its source, that is, who's doing the acting, as this example show:

Passive: The papers will be graded according to the criteria stated in the syllabus.
Active: The teacher will grade the papers according to the criteria stated in the syllabus.

Don't get the idea that the passive voice is always wrong and should never be used. It is a good writing technique when we don't want to be bothered with an obvious or too-often-repeated subject and when we need to rearrange words in a sentence for emphasis.

Revise Subject-verb Mismatches

In dense, highly technical writing, it's easy to lose track of the real subject and pick a verb that just does not make sense. The result is a noun physically not able to do what the verb says it is doing, or some abstract thing performing something nitty-gritty real-world action.

Revise Sentence-length Problems

When you are writing about highly technical subject matter, it is easy to construct long sentences that become hard to read. The military standard for many years has been 17 words per sentence. Other standards allow up to 25 words per sentence. It's not that sentences can't be significantly longer or shorter than these standards-it's just that the average ought to stay somewhere within the 17- to 25-word range. However, any sentence over 35 or 40 words probably needs to be broken up. And while an occasional short sentence (say, 5 to 10 words) can be very effective, lots of them can cause writing to be choppy and hard to follow.

Breaking up overly long sentences is fun-it's a lot like throwing things away or tearing something down. Take a look at these examples, before and after.

17

Abstracts, Introductions, Conclusions

Formal technical reports over eight to ten pages contain several components that deserve their own focus because they are important in technical reports and because people are unfamiliar with them:

— Abstracts provide several kinds of summaries of the report contents and conclusions.

— Introductions get readers ready to read reports by indicating the topic, purpose, intended audience, contents, and orther such matters.

— Conclusions shape how readers view and understand the report upon leaving it.

Abstracts

An abstract is a summary of a body of information. Sometimes, abstracts are in fact called summaries--sometimes, executive summaries or executive abstracts. There are different kinds of abstracts-your technical report uses two types: the descriptive abstract and the informative abstract.

Descriptive Abstracts

The descriptive abstract provides a description of the

report's main topic and purpose as well an overview of its contents. It is very short-usually a brief one- or two-sentence paragraph. It appears on the title page. You may have noticed something similar to this type of abstract at the beginning of journal articles. In this type of abstract, you don't summarize any of the facts or conclusions of the report. The descriptive abstract does not say something .

Informative Abstracts

The informative abstract, as its name implies, provides information from the body of the report-specifically, the key facts and conclusions. To put it another way, this type of abstract summarizes the key information from every major section in the body of the report.

It is as if someone had taken a yellow marker and highlighted all the key points in the body of the report then vaccuumed them up into a one- or two-page document. Specifically, the requirements for the informative abstract are as follows:

— Summarizes the key facts, conclusions, and other important information in the body of the report.

— Usually about 10 percent of the length of the full report: for example, an informative abstract for a 10-page report would be 1 page. This ratio stops after about 30 pages, however. For 50- or 60-page reports, the abstract should not go over 3 to 4 pages.

— Summarizes the key information from each of the main sections of the report, and proportionately so (a 3-page section of a 10-page report ought to take up about 30 percent of the informative abstract).

-- Phrases information in a very dense, compact way. Sentence are longer than normal and are crammed with information. The abstract tries to compact information down to that 10-percent level. It's expected that the writing in an informative abstract will be dense and heavily worded. However, do not omit normal words such as the, a, and an.

— Omits introductory explanation, unless that is the focus of the main body of the report. Definitions and other background information are omitted if they are not the major focus of the report. The informative abstract is not an introduction to the subject matter of the report-and it is not an introduction!

— Omits citations for source borrowings. If you summarize information that you borrowed from other writers, you do not have to repeat the citation in the informative abstract (in other words, no brackets with source numbers and page numbers).

— Includes key statistical detail. Don't sacrifice key numerical facts to make the informative abstract brief. One expects to see numerical data in an informative abstract.

— Omits descriptive-abstract phrasing. You should not see phrasing like this: "This report presents conclusions and recommendations from a survey done on grammar-checking software." Instead, the informative abstract presents the details of those conclusions and recommendations.

This last point is particularly important. People often confuse the kinds of writing expected in descriptive and informative abstracts.

Checklist for Abstracts

As you reread and revise your abstracts, watch out for problems such as the following:

— Make sure that the descriptive abstract does not include informative abstract phrasing; make sure that the informative abstract does not include descriptive abstract phrasing.

— Make sure the descriptive overviews all the contents-all the major sections-of the report.

— Make sure that the informative abstract summarizes all the major sections of the report.

— Make sure the informative abstract summarizes all key concepts, conclusions, and facts from the body of the report (including key statistical information).

— Make sure that the informative abstract excludes general, obvious, deadwood information and that the phrasing is compact and concentrated.

— Make sure that the informative abstract is neither too brief (less than 10 percent) nor too long (more than 15 percent).

Introductions

The introduction is one of the most important sections of a report - or, for that matter, any document - but introductions are often poorly written. One reason may be that people misunderstand the purpose of introductions. An introduction introduces readers to the report and not necessarily, or only minimally, to the subject matter.

Readers have an understandable need to know some basic things about a report before they begin reading it: such as what is it about, why was it written, what's it for, for whom it written, and what are its main contents. Readers need a basic orientation to the topic, purpose, situation, and contents of a report - in other words, an introduction.

Imagine that you were writing a recommendation report about CD-ROM computer devices. You might be tempted to use the introduction to discuss the background of compact disc development or its theoretical side. That might be good stuff to include in the report, and it probably belongs in the report – but not in the introduction, or at least not in much detail or length.

For 10-page, doublespaced reports, introductions might average 1 page. On that one page, you might have three paragraphs, averaging 6 to 8 lines each. One of those paragraphs could be devoted to background information, to introducing the subject matter. But the other two paragraphs must do the job of introducing the report and orienting the reader to the report.

Common Elements

The following is a discussion of the common contents of introductions. Each of these elements is not required in all introductions, and some elements combine into the same sentence. Rather than mechanically applying these elements, write the introduction that seems right to you, then come back and search for these elements in it.

Topic: Somewhere early in the introduction, you need to indicate the specific topic of the report. Some introductions seem to want to hold readers in suspense for a while before they indicate the true topic. That's a bit of a gamble. A better approach is to indicate the topic early--such that you could circle the topic words somewhere in the first three to four lines of the introduction.

Purpose and situation: Somewhere, the report needs to indicate why it was written, for whom, and for what purpose. If the report provides recommendations on whether to implement a program, the introduction needs to indicate that somehow. You might also consider indicating something of the scope of the report--what it is not intended to accomplish.

Audience: The introduction also needs to indicate who are the appropriate or intended readers of the report--for example, "experienced technicians trained on the HAL/ 6000." Also, an introduction should indicate what level of experience or knowledge readers need to understand the report, if any. If none is needed, say that also. If the report was prepared for council members of the City of Utopia, Texas, the introduction needs to express that.

Overview of contents: The introduction to a report should, if nothing else, indicate the main contents of the report. For most reports, some sort of scope indication is also needed in the introduction: some statement about what topics the report does not cover.

Background on the topic: Some minimal background is usually in order for an introduction – for example, some key definitions, some historical background, some theory, something on the importance of the subject. Information like this gets readers interested, motivated to read, grounded in some fundamental concepts. Watch out, though – this discussion can get away from you and fill up more than page. If it does, that's okay; all is not lost. That just shows the information is important and should be in the report – just not in the introduction.

Background on the situation: Another kind of background is also a good candidate for introductions--the situation that brought about the need for the report. For example, if there were a lot of conflicting data about some new technology or some problem, which brought about the need for the research, this background could be summarized in the introduction. For example, if a company needed new equipment of some kind or if the company had some problem or need and some requirements in relation to that equipment--discussion of these matters should go in the introduction.

Notice in the discussion of these elements the word "indicate" keeps getting used. That's because you'd like to avoid heavy-handed language such as "The topic of this report is..." or "This report has been written for..." Often there are nicer ways to express these things. For example, if your report is about grammar-checking software, just make sure that phrase occurs at some appropriate place early in the introduction--you don't need to drone something like "The topic of this report is grammar-checking software..." Of course, if this direct approach is the only or the best way to express it, then do it! Notice in the example introductions that this kind of phrasing does occur.

Section Introductions

We don't normally think that there is more than one introduction in a report. However, in reports over 8 to 10 or more pages, the individual sections also need some sort of introduction. These can be called section introductions because they prepare you to read a section of a report--they orient you to its contents and purpose. Of course, a section introduction has nothing like the elements of the report introduction. However, it does have several that, if handled well, can make a lot of difference in the clarity and flow of a report.

Topic indication: As with the report introduction, indicate the topic of the upcoming section. But remember – it doesn't have to be the stodgy, heavy-handed "The topic of this next section of the report is..."

Contents overview: Just as in the report introduction, it is a good idea to list the main contents. The in-sentence list serves this purpose well.

Transition: An element that is very useful in section introductions but unnecessary in report introductions is the transitional phrasing that indicates how the preceding section is related to the one about to start. In reports of any length and complexity, it is a good technique--it guides readers along, showing them how the parts of the report all fit together.

Checklist for Introductions

As you revise your introductions, watch out for problems such as the following:

— Avoid writing an introduction consisting of only background information; avoid allowing background information to overshadow the key elements of the introduction.

— Make sure the topic of the report is indicated early.

— Be sure to indicate the audience and situation--what the readers should expect from the report; what knowledge or background they need to understand the report; what situation brought about the need for the report.

— Make sure there is an overview of the report contents, plus scope information--what the report doesn't cover.

Conclusions

We normally use the word "conclusion" to refer to that last section or paragraph or a document. Actually, however, the word refers more to a specific type of final section. If we were going to be fussy about it, this section should be called "Final Sections."

There seem to be at least four ways to end a report: a summary, a true conclusion, an afterword, and nothing. Yes, it is possible to end a document with no conclusion (or "final section") whatsoever. However, in most cases, that's a bit like slamming the phone down without even saying good-bye. More often, the final section is some combination of the first three ways of ending the document.

One common way to wrap up a report is to review and summarize the high points. If your report is rather long, complex, heavily detailed, and if you want your readers to come away with the right perspective, a summary is in order. For short reports, summaries can seem absurd–the reader thinks "You've just told me that!" Summaries need to read as if time has passed, things have settled down, and the writer is viewing the subject from higher ground.

True Conclusions

A "true" conclusion is a logical thing. For example, in the body of a report, you might present conflicting theories and explored the related data. Or you might have compared different models and brands of some product. In the conclusion, the "true" conclusion, you'd present your interpretation, your choice of the best model or brand--your final conclusions.

Afterwords

One last possibility for ending a report involves turning to some related topic but discussing it at a very general level. Imagine that you had written a background report on some exciting new technology. In the final section, you might broaden your focus and discuss how that technology might be used, or the problems it might bring about. But the key is to keep it general--don't force yourself into a whole new detailed section.

Combinations

In practice, these ways of ending reports combine. You can analyze final sections of reports and identify elements that summarize, elements that conclude, and elements that discuss something related but at a general level. Here are some possibilities for afterword-type final sections:

- Provide a brief, general look to the future; speculate on future developments.
- Explore solutions to problems that were discussed in the main body of the report.
- Discuss the operation of a mechanism or technology that was discussed in the main body of the report.
- Provide some cautions, guidelines, tips, or preview of advanced functions at the end of a set of instructions.

— Explore the economics, social implications, problems, legal aspects, advantages, disadvantages, benefits, or applications of the report subject (but only generally and briefly).

Revision Checklist for Conclusions

As you reread and revise your conclusions, watch out for problems such as the following:

— If you use an afterword-type last section, make sure you write it at a general enough level that it doesn't seem like yet another body section of the report.

— Avoid perfunctory conclusions that have no real reason to be in the report.

— Keep final sections brief and general.

Organizational Policies and Procedures

Organizations use policies and procedures documents to record their rules and regulations. These can include whatever the organizations considers important for its operations: attendance policies, substance-abuse policies, work-flow procedures, and so on. Once recorded, the policies and procedures are there for everybody in the organization to refer to, and these documents become the means of settling most disputes within the organization.

To distinguish between these two terms, policies are general statements of how an organization want things to be within its walls. For example, it may have a policy that dictates eager, aggressive, do-whatever-takes customer support. But to make that policy a working reality, it will also have one or more procedures that define exactly what to do - step by step - when a customer calls with a complaint or problem.

If you are enrolled in a course associated with this page, you are in a writing course, not a business-policy course. Our focus is on good writing, well-designed documents, documents that accomplish their purpose, and documents that meet common expectations as to their content, organization, and format. Policies and procedures are obviously an important application of writing and can contain substantial technical information about a business's operations. That's why it's a good option for the final project in a technical-writing course.

You can write policies and procedures if you need to write such a document for an actual business or organization, if you are working for an organization that lacks them, or if you'd merely like to do some constructive daydreaming about how an organization ought to be structured. Beware, however, if you are just playing around with this notion: the policies and procedures you write for this course must be every bit as serious, realistic, specific, factual, well-researched, and well-thought-out as policies and procedures for a real situation.

Policies and procedures can be very large documents containing information that you may have no way of getting. Work with your instructor to reach an agreement on the scope of the document you write. Remember too that your instructor is probably not a professional business or organizational consultant and probably won't be able to help you on the finer points of your policies and procedures document.

For this unit, CCH Incorporated has kindly agreed to let us link to its SOHO Guidebook: A Practical Guide to Starting, Running and Growing a Small Business. There is a loosely defined category of reports that is very important in technical writing. These reports are variously called feasibility reports, recommendation reports, evaluation reports, assessment reports, and who knows what else. They all do roughly the same thing—provide carefully studied opinions and, sometimes, recommendations. There are some subtle differences among some these types, but there are absolutely no universally agreed-upon names for them:

— *Feasibility report*: This type studies a situation (for example, a problem or opportunity) and a plan for doing something about it and then determines whether that plan is "feasible"--which means determining whether it technologically possible and whether it is practical (in terms of current technology, economics, social needs, and so on). The feasibility report answers the question "Should we implement Plan X?" by stating "yes," "no," but more often "maybe." Not only does it give a recommendation, it also provides the data and the reasoning behind that recommendation.

— *Recommendation report*: This type starts from a stated need, a selection of choices, or both and then recommends one, some, or none. For example, a company might be looking at grammar-checking software and want a recommendation on which product is the best. You could study the market for this type of application and recommend one particular product, a couple of products (differing perhaps in their strengths and their weaknesses), or none (maybe none of them are any good). The recommendation report answers the question "Which option should we choose?" (or in some cases "Which are the best options?) by recommending Product B, or maybe both Products B and C, or none of the products.

— *Evaluation report*: This type provides an opinion or judgment rather than a yes-no-maybe answer or a recommendation. It provides a studied opinion on the value or worth of something. For example, for over a year the city of Austin had free bus transportation in an attempt to increase ridership and reduce automobile traffic. Did it work? Was it worthwhile?--These are questions an evaluation report would attempt to answer. This type of report compares a thing to a set of requirements (or criteria) and determines how well it meets those requirements.

As you can see, these distinctions are rather fine; and they overlap. In real-world writing, these types often combine – you might see elements of the recommendation report combine with the feasibility report, for example. Of course, the writers of these reports don't care which type they are writing – and well they shouldn't! They're trying to get a job done.

Typical Contents

Whatever shade of feasibility or recommendation report you write, whatever name people call it--most of the sections and the organization of those sections are roughly the same. Your specific writing project may not require all of these sections, nor in the order shown here--plus you may need other sections not mentioned here.

The structural principle fundamental to this type of report is this: you provide not only your recommendation, choice, or judgment, but also the data and the conclusions leading up to it. That way, readers can check your findings, your logic, and your conclusions and come up with a completely different view. But, more likely, they will be convinced by all your careful research and documentation.

Introduction: In the introduction, indicate that the document that follows is a feasibility report (or whatever it is called). Instead of calling the report by name (which might not mean anything to most readers), you can indicate its purpose. Also, provide an overview of the contents of the report.

For some feasibility reports, you'll also be able to discuss the situation and the requirements in the introductions. If there is little to say about them, you can merge them with the introduction, or make the introduction two paragraphs long.

Technical Background: Some feasibility reports may require some technical discussion in order to make the rest of the report meaningful to readers. The dilemma with this kind of information is whether to put it in a section of its own or to fit it into the comparison sections where it is relevant. For example, a discussion of power and speed of laptop computers is going to necessitate some discussion of RAM, megahertz, and processors. Should you put that in a section that compares the laptops according to power and speed? Should you keep the comparison neat and clean, limited strictly to the comparison and the conclusion? Maybe all the technical background can be pitched in its own section--either toward the front of the report or in an appendix.

Background on the Situation: For many feasibility reports, you'll need to discuss the problem, need. If there is little that needs to be said about it, this information can go in the introduction.

Requirements and Criteria: A critical part of feasibility and recommendation reports is the discussion of the requirements you'll use to reach the final decision or recommendation. If you're trying to recommend a laptop computer for use by employees, there are likely to be requirements concerning size, cost, hard-disk storage, display quality, durability, and battery function. If you're looking into the feasibility of providing every ACC student with an ID on the ACC computer network, you'd need define the basic requirements of such a program--what it would be expected to accomplish, problems that it would have to avoid, and so on. If you're evaluating the recent program of free bus transporation in Austin, you'd need to know what was expected of the program and then compare its actual results to those requirements.

Requirements can be defined in several basic ways:

— *Numerical values*: Many requirements are stated as maximum or minimum numerical values. For example, there may be a cost requirement--the laptop should cost no more than $900.

— *Yes/no values*: Some requirements are simply a yes-no question. Does the laptop come equipped with a modem? Is the car equipped with air conditioning?

— *Ratings values*: In some cases, key considerations cannot be handled either with numerical values or yes/no values. For example, we might want a laptop that has an ease-of-use rating of at least "good" by some nationally accepted ratings group. Or we may have to assign a rating ourselves.

The term "requirements" is used here instead of "criteria." A certain amount of ambiguity hangs around this word; plus most people are not sure whether it is singular or plural. (Technically, it is plural; "criterion" is singular, although "criteria" is commonly used for both the singular and plural. Try using "criterion" in public--you'll get weird looks. "Criterias" is not a word and should never be used.)

The requirements section should also discuss how important the individual requirements are in relation to each other. Picture the typical situation where no one option is best in all categories of comparison. One option is cheaper; another has more functions; one has better ease-of-use ratings; another is known to be more durable. Devise a method by which you can pick a "winner" from situation where there is no clear winner.

Discussion of the Options: In certain kinds of feasibility or recommendation reports, you'll need to explain how you narrowed the field of choices down to the ones your report focuses on. Often, this follows right after the discussion of the requirements. Your basic requirements may well narrow the field down for you. But there may be other considerations that disqualify other options--explain these as well.

Additionally, you may need to provide brief descriptions of the options themselves. Don't get this mixed up with the comparison that comes up in the next section.

In this description section, you provide a general discussion of the options so that readers will know something about them. The discussion at this stage is not comparative. It's just a general orientation to the options. In the laptops example, you might want to give some brief, general specifications on each model about to be compared.

Category-by-Category Comparisons: One of the most important parts of a feasibility or recommendation report is the comparison of the options. Remember that you include this section so that readers can check your thinking and come up with different conclusions if they desire. This should be handled category by category, rather than option by option. If you were comparing laptops, you'd have a section that compared them on cost, another section that compared them on battery function, and so on. You wouldn't have a section that discussed everything about option A, another that discussed everything about option B, and so on. That would not be effective at all, because the comparisons must still be made somewhere.

Each of these comparative sections should end with a conclusion that states which option is the best choice in that particular category of comparison. Of course, it won't always be easy to state a clear winner--you may have to qualify the conclusions in various ways, providing multiple conclusions for different conditions. If you were doing an evaluation report, you obviously wouldn't be comparing options. Instead, you'd be comparing the thing being evaluated against the requirements placed upon it, the expectations people had of it.

18 Indexing

As a technical writer typically have to create indexes for the print books and for online helps you develop. The type of index we mean here is the classic back-of-book index that shows page numbers on which topics and subtopics occur within the book. An online index is much the same except that you supply hypertext links rather than page numbers. The following gives a relatively quick system for creating a thorough,. functional index, for either print or online

Rough-Drafting an Index

As with any writing project, there is a rough-drafting phase for indexing. And of course, you need to think about your audience - who they are, how they'll use the index, why they'll use it, and what sorts of terminology they might be accustomed to. After that, here's what to do next:

Convert each heading into multiple index entries: Headings are a good place to start: they indicate topics and subtopics - precisely what an index does. However, don't just copy headings directly into an index. Tools like RoboHELP and FrameMaker lure you into this trap - just don't go there. Instead, "clone" each headings as many times as you can.

For example, a heading such as "Changing screen resolution" can be indexed as "screen resolution, changing" as well as "changing screen resolution." You might also include "resolution, changing screen." These cloned entries attempt to anticipate all the likely ways a reader might look for this topic in an index: "screen," "resolution," or "changing."

You can't always clone index entries on every word. For example, "introducing streaming multimedia" in the preceding just wouldn't work.

Create synonym entries: Readers don't necessary use the same terminology as you do in your documentation. They may call a diskette drive a "floppy drive." They may refer to a display as a "monitor." As an indexer, you must anticipate these common variations in terminology. In the preceding entries, it would be a good idea to have a synonym for "video display" such as "monitor." But instead of repeating the page numbers, use a See reference. That way, you point readers to the preferred term. (Of course, if there is only one page number, just repeat it with the synonym entry.)

Some additional examples:

Index entry	Synynom entries
volume, adjusting	loudness, adjusting
transmission rate	speed, transmission
capturing video	copying video

Review the text for additional index entries: It's ordinarily not enough just to index by headings. You have to dig down in the text for concepts, terms, and tasks that are not represented by the headings. For example, under the heading "Creating a Multimedia Stream," you might see definitions of "capturing" and "encoding." These are important terms, but they appear nowhere in the headings - index them too! In this case, you'd want to create these additional index entries: "capturing streams" and "encoding streams."

Index front and back matter: Don't forget to dig around in the preface, safety notices, appendixes, and other such peripherals for additional index entries. Typically, technical-support numbers and addresses are shown in the preface. Index them - and don't forget to create cloned entries and synonym entries for them as well.

Index entry	Cloned and synynom entries
technical support	support, technical help deskproblems

Revising and Finetuning an Index

Once you've brainstormed all the index entries that you can think of, it's time to see what the thing looks like and start working it over. to revise a rough-draft index:

Build a first-draft index: Once you've created as many index entries, clones, and synonyms as you can, it's time to "build" a first draft of the index. Unless you are working the old-fashioned way with index cards, you can get your software application to do this for you. For example, if you work in FrameMaker, you've gone through your text inserting index entries. The same process applies to RoboHELP. When you build the first-draft index, don't be dismayed. It's just a rough draft, which you'll need to do several kinds of revision to.

Toss useless entries: In the preceding steps, you've been rough-drafting the index. In the phase, you don't get hung up about the exact phrasing of entries or the likelihood that anybody would ever use them. But now the time to start weeding out the entries that no reader would ever use. For example, first-level entries beginning with "introducing," "using, "about" are not likely to be useful. Delete them! But don't delete them from the built index. Go back into your document and get rid of the original index entry.

Consolidate entries with similar phrasing. You'll also find lots of enries that have only minor variations in phrasing. For example:

Rough-draft entries	Revised entries
technology, streaming multimedia	technologies, streaming multimedia
technologies, streaming multimedia	
video display	video displays
video displays	
change screen resolution	changing screen resolution
changing screen resolution	

As you can see in these examples, singular/plural entries and verb variations are the most common causes of similar phrasing in index entries. Your house style may dictate using singulars as opposed to plural. Whichever way you handle these, just be consistent.

Group similar entries: You'll also see entries that need to be grouped and subordinated. For example, they may all begin with the same word, but have different modifiers. Here's an example:

Similar entries	Grouped and subordinated entries
projector, defined	projectors
projectors, compiling	compiling
projectors, compiling	considerations
projectors, considerations	creating
projectors, creating	defined
projectors, troubleshooting	troubleshooting

Rework entries with over excessive page entries: Some organizations have actual style-guide rules concerning how many page references following an index entry are allowable. Three is a common maximum; two is aggressive, ambitious. For example, "programming syntax, 12, 45, 74, 122, 219, 222." A string of anonymous page references like this helps no one. Instead, identify the subtopic for these page references.

Look for entry groupings: A nice useful touch in indexes is to hunt for ways that you can group entries.

Look for See also and additional See references: Toward the end of your revising phase, take a look at your index for the possibility of See also references. See also references are for closely related terms that readers might choose by mistake. For example, in the old DOS systems, there was the copy command and the xcopy command. The two commands are so closely related in name and in function that you'd want to put See also references to each other.

Check the style and mechanics of index entries: The organization for which you work may have its own house style guide or refer you to some standard style such as the Chicago Manual of Style. Look at these very carefully for how they tell you to capitalize and punctuate index entries. Indexes commonly use lowercase on all nonproper-noun entries, but a certain percentage do use initial caps on first-level entries. Most styles have you put a comma just after the index term and before the page numbers; but a few do not. Some styles require you to use the same highlighting in the index as you do in the main text. If something is bold in the main text, they want it bold in the index too.

19

Libraries, Documentation, Cross-referencing

The big issue when you begin your library search is finding those words and phrases that enable you to find the books, articles, reports, and encyclopedias that have all that information you need. A keyword (also called a "descriptor") is a word or phrase under which related information sources are listed. Imagine you're writing a report on the latest theories about the greenhouse effect: you'd check book catalogs and periodical indexes for "greenhouse effect," hoping to find lists of books or articles under that keyword.

But that might not be the right one; things might be listed under the keyword "global warming" instead. So how do you find the right keywords? Here are some suggestions:

— Brainstorm like crazy! Imagine the possibilities for artificial intelligence: computer-simulated intelligence? machine intelligence? Of course, as it turns out, one big area of this field is called neural networks--who would ever think of that? That's why you need to try some other possibilities as well.

— Try to find someone who is familiar with your topic; explore how they refer to it.

— Take a look in the Library of Congress Subject Headings. This a giant, multi-volume set of keywords. Big problem with it is that it is not updated and reissued often. If you've got a new-technology topic, it may not be much help.

— Try using a system called Dynix: type in your search word followed by two questions marks, and it will give a list of possibilities (ask an ACC librarian for help on this one).

— Try to find any book or article on your topic – anything. Then explore it for the vocabulary it uses. In particular, check its listings for titles of other books and articles.

If you faithfully go through the following suggestions, you're likely to have a long list of books, article, reports, and other sources – more than you could ever read in one semester. First of all, don't back away from at least knowing what's "out there" on your topic.

Once you start looking at your list, you'll see many things that seem to duplicate each other. If, for example, you have five or six books with roughly the same title, just pick the one that is the most recent and that seems the most complete and thorough. Many other sources will branch out into subtopics you have no interest in. And of course many of the items won't even be available in any nearby library or bookstore.

All you really need are those one or two books, those two or three articles, several encyclopedia articles – that's your "critical mass" that you can begin working with. You consult the items on your big list only when you run into areas that seem controversial and areas where the information seems contradictory, confusing, or just too vague.

Information Sources

Once you've convinced yourself that you need to go after

some external information sources and have found some pretty reliable keywords to use, it's time to start the search. The logical starting point is whichever information source you think is likely to have the best stuff. For hot, late-breaking topics, articles and proceedings may be the best bet. For stable topics that have been around awhile, books and encyclopedias may be better. However, if you're not sure, you may want to systematically check a number of the common types of information sources.

Internet Resources

It's increasingly possible to do much if not all your information gathering on the Internet and particularly through the World Wide Web. Take a look at these web resources for information searching.

Books

One good starting place for your information search is books. At ACC, there are three immediately available resources you can use to find books:

— First, there is ACC's online book catalog. Check it using as many different keywords that are related to your topic as you can think of. (See the discussion in "Descriptors and keywords," starting page B-1, for information on finding these.) As you find potentially useful titles, print them (most of the ACC library displays are hooked up to printers).

— Another step you should take is to check the UT book catalog. No, you don't have to drive to UT; the ACC library has a computer that is logged into the UT catalog. Go search it with the same keywords you searched the ACC catalog. And again, print out your results on the printer that is attached to the computer.

— Another useful strategy for finding books is to check Books in Print, in particular, the online version that is issued on CD-ROM (the ACC library has the books only). Use your keywords here also.

If you do all these searches, you're likely to end up with a monster list of books. No, you don't have to read every one of them. In fact, you may not be able to lay your hands on most of them. Check the list and try to find a book that seems the most recent and the most definitive. And, no, you don't have to read all of it either – just the parts that relate directly to your topic.

As soon as you can, try to get your hands on as many of these books as you can. Check their bibliographies (list of books, articles, and other information sources consulted) at the end of the book, at the ends of chapters, and in footnotes. These will be good leads to other books that your other searches may not have found. Also, while you're in the stacks, check the books nearby the ones you have on your list; you may see other ones that could prove useful.

Journal Articles and Magazine

While books give you fairly stable information and often at a higher level of generality, magazines, journals, and newspapers often give you much more specific, up-to-date information. There are two ways to approach finding journal articles: through general indexes and through specialized indexes. Here are some strategies for finding articles:

— Check several general indexes for your topic. These indexes cover a broad range of magazines and journals--they are more popular and are for general audiences and therefore can't be relied on specialized, technical material. Still, they are a great place to start, and if you are not being very technically ambitious with your report, they may supply you with all you need. At ACC, the general indexes include Reader's Guide to Periodical Literature. Try finding your topic in the most recent volume of each of these.

— Try to find a good specialized index for the field that is related to your topic. At ACC, try UMI Periodicals Abstracts, Academic Abstracts, Social Issues Research Series, Business Periodicals Index, General Science Index, Public Affairs Information Service (PAIS), and Applied Science and Technology Index. Again check for your topic in an appropriate volume of whichever of these indexes you use.

Once you get a list of promising articles, don't assume that ACC has them all. If you use Academic Abstracts or UMI Periodicals Abstracts, there's a greater chance that ACC will. If ACC doesn't have a periodical you need, check the listing of UT periodicals.

As with books, you won't be able to read all of the articles you find, nor will you even be able to get access to them (or at least right away). Try finding and reading the abstracts of the article on your list; this is a good way to get a brief picture of what the article contains and whether it will be useful to you. Just try to find the articles that relate directly to your topic, and read them selectively when you get them.

Encyclopedias

Another good source of introductory information is encyclopedias. You can use these either to get yourself up to speed to read and understand the more technical information you come across, or you can use the encyclopedia information itself in your report.

— Check for your topic in a general encyclopedia, using all the various keywords related to that topic you can think of. As with periodical indexes, encyclopedias are available in general and specialized varieties. You're familiar with the general encyclopedias such as World Book Encyclopedia and the Britannica.

And of course a number of encyclopedias are now available online in CD-ROM format (however, the content of most of these seems rather slight compared to the printed versions). These are great for starters, and in some cases they may provide all the information you need in your report. Also, check any bibliography--lists of related books, articles, and reports--that may be listed at the end of individual articles.

— Also try to find an appropriate specialized, or technical encyclopedia in which to search for your topic. You may need more technical detail, or your topic may be a tough one not covered very well in general information sources- in which case you may want to consult specialized encyclopedias.

Even in this group, there are general ones that cover a broad range of scientific and technical fields – one well-entrenched one is the McGraw-Hill Encyclopedia of Science and Technology. Another one is VanNostrand's Scientific Encyclopedia. Look for your topic in these. Again, check the bibliographies at the end of the articles you consult. These may point you to articles, books, and reports that will be useful in your report work.

But there are even more specialized encyclopedias – ones focusing directly on a field or profession, for example, solar energy, computers, biology, nursing, and so on. If you can find these, you may be able to zero in on your topic even more – and once again, be sure to check out the lists of other sources at the end of the articles. For help in finding these specialized encyclopedias, check with a librarian.

Reference books – handbooks, guides, atlases, dictionaries, yearbooks. Another source of information reports is all those reference books out there. Every field has its handbooks (repositories of relatively stable, "basic" information in the field), guides (information on literature in the field, associations, legalities, and so on), atlases (more than just maps, great repositories of statistical data), dictionaries and encyclopedias, and finally yearbooks (articles, data, and summaries of the year's activity in a given field). The ACC library has many of these kinds of reference books, and the UT library has even more. If you browse around the reference area of the ACC library, you'll see titles such as these:

— Prentice-Hall Encyclopedia of Information Technology

— McGraw-Hill Dictionary of the Life Sciences

— Robotics Sourcebook and Dictionary

— Energy: A Guide to Organizations and Information Resources in the United States

— McGraw-Hill Yearbook of Science and Technology

One enormous source of technical information is the U.S. government. The only problem is getting to the indexes of it, and then getting the documents themselves. If you're willing to make a trip to the UT main (Perry-Castaneda) library or to the Texas State Library (just east of the Capitol), you can get at most of both.

Both libraries are like dumpsites for selected U.S. government documents–and that amounts to a lot! And of course many of these documents are on various kinds of microforms in order to conserve space. But if you wanted a pile of technical reports related to your topic, you could get them this way. Try these strategies for checking in government documents for your topic:

— Check in a recent volume of Congressional Indexing Service for reports on your topic (be sure to read the companion abstracts).

— Check a recent volume of the Government Reports and Announcements index for reports and other information sources related to your topic.

— Check Index to U.S. Government Periodicals for articles appearing in U.S. government magazines and journals related to your topic.

These sources give you just a taste of what's available in government documents. Better indexed methods of finding this type of information are probably now available; check with a librarian for help.

Information from non-profit, association sources. One interesting and nonacademic strategy for finding information is to check for interest groups and trade associations that may be related in some way to your report topic. While there are probably many different ways of finding organizations like these, the Encyclopedia of Associations is one readily available way. Use its topic listings to find your topic (remembering to check all possible keywords), make a list of organizations you find. Some of these will be glad to send you information – although it will likely be strongly biased toward their particular viewpoint. If you have enough time, write inquiry letters to a few of these organizations, and see what additional information you can get.

Information Searches

Try following each of these suggestions to see what sorts of information you can find for your topic:

— Using Library of Congress Subject Headings, list as many related keywords (subject headings, descriptors) for your topic as you can.

— Using each of your keywords, search the ACC and UT online catalogs for books related to your topic.

— Check Books in Print: Subjects for books on your topic (using your keywords).

— Check one or two annual volumes of Reader's Guide to Periodical Literature for articles on your topic (again, using your keywords).

— Use Academic Abstracts, Social Sciences Research Issues, or both to check for articles. (These are online databases; you can print out your results.)

— If applicable, check for articles on your topic in one or two volumes of Applied Science and Technology Index, General Science Index, Business Periodicals Index, Public Affairs Information Service (PAIS) – any that apply to your topic.

— Check one volume of the New York Times Index for newspaper articles on your topic.

— Check ACC's online magazine and journal index for articles on your topic (and print out your results).

— Check a general encyclopedia for articles related to your topic.

— Try to find a specialized encyclopedia related to your topic; look for articles on your topic in it. (In particular, check in McGraw-Hill Encyclopedia of Science and Technology).

— Try to find a yearbook related in some way to your topic and see what information it has on your topic. (In particular, check two or three volumes of the McGraw-Hill Yearbook of Science and Technology.)

— Find Encyclopedia of Associations and look for interest groups, trade associations, and other kinds of organizations that might have something to do with your topic.

— Using the information sources you actually find, check the bibliographies at the ends of books and articles and the ends of chapters in books, as well as the footnotes, for additional information sources.

Number System of Documentation

If you've taken other college writing courses recently, you have probably been exposed to other documentation systems-specifically the MLA, or works-cited system. The problem with that system is that it is used rather narrowly in the literature field. Unfortunately, it is not widely used outside that field-especially not in technical and scientific fields. One of the more common systems used in technical fields is the number system. It's too bad you have to learn a different system, but at least this one is easy to learn and use.

ACC libraries have a handout entitled CBE (Scientific) Documentation-this is one of the specific incarnations of the number system; get a copy in case the information here does not cover your needs. In the number system, you list your information sources alphabetically, number them, and put the list at the back of your report. Then in the body of your report, whenever you borrow information from one of those sources, you put the source number and, optionally, the page number in brackets at that point in the text where the borrowed information occurs.

It's a bit tricky deciding exactly where to place the source indicators-at the beginning of the passage containing the borrowed information, at the end? If it makes sense to "attribute" the source, you can put the attribution at the beginning and the bracketed source indicator at the end.

Number documentation system: the code numbers in the text of the report are keyed to the references page. For example, [6:5] in the middle of the page from the body of the report indicates that the information came from source 6 (in References), page 5. Notice the attribution of the quotation marks the beginning of the borrowed information and the bracketed source indicator marks the end.

Sources List

A bit more challenging is setting up the list of information sources-that numbered, alphabetized list you put at the end of the document. The best thing to do is use examples. The following illustrations show you how to handle books, government reports, article from magazines and journals, encyclopedia articles, and personal interviews.

Internet and Web information sources: For format on citing Internet and Web information sources, see the Columbia Guide to Online Style.

Books: For books, put the name of the author (first name last) first, followed by a period, followed by the title of the book (in italics if you have; otherwise, underline), followed by a period, followed by the city of the publisher, followed by a colon, followed by the publisher's name (but delete all those tacky "Inc.," "Co.," and "Ltd." things), followed by the year of publication, ending with a period. In this style, you don't indicate pages.

Magazine and journal articles: Start with the author's name first (last name first), followed by a period, then the title of the article in quotation marks and ending with a period, followed by the name of the magazine or journal (in italics if you have it; otherwise, underline), followed by a period, followed by the date of issue of the magazine the article occurs in, followed by the beginning and ending page. If the article spread out across the magazine, you can write "33+." or "33(5)." The latter style seems to be taking hold; in it, you estimate how many pages the article would be if it were continuous.

If there is no author, start with the article or book title. If there are two authors, add "and" and the second author's name, first name first. If there are too many authors, use the first one (last name first), followed by "et al.," which means "and others."

Encyclopedia articles: Encyclopedia articles are easy! Start with the title of the article in quotation marks ending with a period, followed by the name of the encyclopedia (in italics if you have it; otherwise, underline), followed by the period, then the year of the edition of the encyclopedia.

Reports: With reports, you're likely to dealing with government reports or local informally produced reports. With most reports, you may not have an individual author name; in such cases, you use the group name as the author. For government reports, the publisher is often the Government Printing Office; and the city of publication, Washington, D.C. Also, for government documents, you should include the document number.

Personal interviews, correspondence, and other nonprint sources: With these sources, you treat the interviewee or letter writer as the author, follow that name with the person's title, followed by a period, then the company name, followed by a period, then the city and state, followed by a period, then what the information was followed by a period, ending with the date.

Product brochures: For these kinds of information sources, treat the company name as the author, followed by a period, use something identifying like the product name (including the specific model number), followed by anything that seems like the title of the brochure, followed by a period, ending with a date if you can find one.

Documenting borrowed graphics: It's certainly legal to copy graphics from other sources and use them in your own work-as long as you document them. You indicate the source of a borrowed graphic in the figure title, which is located just below the graphic. In the figure title, you can show the source of the graphic in two ways-the long traditional way and a shorter way that uses the format of the number system.

Cross-referencing

Technical reports and instructions often require cross-references – those pointers to other places in the same document or to other information sources where related information can be found.

Cross-references can help readers in a number of different ways. It can point them toward more basic information if, for example, they have entered into a report over their heads. It can point them to more advanced information if, for example, they already know the stuff you're trying to tell them. Also, it can point them to related information.

Related information is the hardest area to explain because ultimately everything is related to everything else – there could be no end to the cross-references. But here's an example from DOS – that troll that lurks inside PC-type computers and supposedly helps you. There are several ways you can copy files: the COPY command, the DISKCOPY command, and XCOPY command. Each method offers different advantages. If you were writing about the COPY command, you'd want cross-references to these other two so that readers could do a bit of shopping around.

Of course, the preceding discussion assumed cross-references within the same document. If there is just too much background to cover in your report, you can cross-reference some external book or article that does provide that background. That way, you are off the hook for having to explain all that stuff. Now, a decent cross-reference consists of several elements:

— Name of the source being referenced: This can either be the title or a general subject reference. If it is a chapter title or a heading, put it in quotation marks; if it is the name of a book, magazine, report, or reference work, put it in italics or underline.

— *Page number*: Required if it is in the same document; optional if it is to another document.

— *Subject matter of the cross-reference*: Often, you need to state what's in the cross-referenced material and indicate why the reader should go to the trouble of checking it out.

Bibliography

C.V. Carey, *Mind the Stop: A brief guide to punctuation and a note on proof-correction*, first published Cambridge University Press, 1939.

Charles T. Brusaw et al, *Handbook of Technical Writing*, Fifth Edition, New York: St. Martin's Press, 1997.

Daniel Anderson, Bret Benjamin, Bill Paredes-Holt, *Connections: a guide to on-line writing*, Boston: Allyn and Bacon, 1998, pp.331, ISBN: 0205268471

Gerald J. Alred et al, *The Professional Writer*, New York: St Martin's Press, 1992.

Hy Bender, *Essential Software for Writers: a complete guide for everyone who writes with a PC*, Cincinnati, OH: Writer's Digest Books, 1993, pp.486, ISBN: 0898796679

Jo Billingham, *Editing and Revising Text*, Oxford: Oxford University Press, 2002, pp.144 , ISBN 0198604130

Jonathan Anderson and Millicent Poole, *Thesis and Assignment Writing*, London: John Wiley, 1994.

Naomi S. Baron, *Alphabet to Email: How Written English Evolved and Where It's Heading*, London/New York: Routledge, 2000, pp.316, ISBN: 0415186854

Ralph Berry, *The Research Project: how to write it*, Routledge, third edition, 1994.

Rita S. Brause, *Writing your Doctoral Dissertation: Invisible Rules for Success*, London and New York: Falmer Press, 2000, pp.163, ISBN 0750707445.

Robert Allen, *Punctuation*, Oxford: Oxford University Press, 2002, pp.128 , ISBN 0198604394

————————, *Spelling*, Oxford: Oxford University Press, 2002, pp.128, ISBN 0198603835

Robert Barrass, *Students Must Write: A Guide to Better Writing in Coursework and Examinations*, London: Routledge, second edition 1995, pp.194, ISBN 0415132223

————————, *Writing at Work: A guide to better writing in administration*, business and management, London: Routledge, 2002, pp.201, ISBN 0415267536

William Condon and Wayne Butler, *Writing the Information SuperHighway*, Boston: Allyn and Bacon, 1997, pp.318, ISBN: 020519575X

Index